PEARLS FROM
THE INFINITE WISDOM

The Art of Self Inquiry.

Volume 1

By

Swami Amritachitswarūpananda Puri

Mata Amritanandamayi Center
San Ramon, California, USA

PEARLS FROM THE INFINITE WISDOM
The Art of Self Inquiry.

Volume 1

Swami Amritachitswarūpananda Puri

Published by:
Mata Amritanandamayi Center
P.O. Box 613
San Ramon, CA 94583-0613, USA

First Edition, May 2022

In India:
    www.amritapuri.org
    inform@amritapuri.org

In Europe:
    www.amma-europe.org

In US:
    www.amma.org

Table of Contents

Foreword

"The ability to retain equanimity of mind in all circumstances is what makes a successful life" -Amma

The content of this book is based on a series of letters written by Swami Amritachitswarūpananda Puri. The Swami, a sanyasi at the Mata Amritanandamayi Math in Amritapuri, Kerala, while performing his earthly duties as a physician at the ashram, took the time to share his experiences through letters and now to a larger spiritual audience through this book. He conveys to us the essence of Vedanta through simple, easily understandable arguments that we can verify through our own intellect. Many of us spend years or even decades in spiritual practices such as seva, charity, japa, meditation and still feel that we have not yet attained real peace. By using Amma's teachings, the Swami explains how the presence of God is to be practiced by shifting our identification (currently rooted in the body and mind) to Brahman (Self). "The various sadhanas of seva, karma yoga, japa, meditation, etc help us gain clarity and concentration of mind. To realize the truth, we must discard the body-mind-world perspective, and instead see from the standpoint of the Self. The ego, which is imagined to be our true Self due to ignorance, should be seen and understood as non-existent and unreal by focussing on the knowledge about our real nature."

When the Swami asked me to review the book, not only did I acutely feel my lack of qualification to do so, but I was also not spiritually inclined to the path of Pure jñāna or knowledge, being a long-time follower of Srimad Bhagavatam. However as

I went through the chapters, through God's grace, I was able to grasp the content of the book as expressed through Amma's teachings using her quotes and Swami's exposition of Vedanta. The effect is the ability to happily remain unperturbed with the ups and downs of life and go about joyfully with life.

The book is interspersed with quotes from Amma's enlightening teachings providing a guiding light to Swami's spiritual message. While Amma's teachings in the quotes remain succinct, sweet, and focus on the main principles, Swami elaborates on them diving deep into the intellectual aspects of Vedanta and presenting convincing arguments from the Srutis on the Truth that our real nature is the Sat-Chit-Ananda itself and that the Real 'I' is untouched by the world around us.

The Swami stresses, again and again, the futility of pursuing Artha and Kāma as they are nothing but unreal appearances on the changeless Self. Hearing these words from Amma and the Swami is a great way to strengthen our conviction that we are nothing but that blissful Self and to develop the courage to cast off the notion that we are individuals with name and form. God imparts us this knowledge through love and draws us within and makes us one with the Universal Being that God is. May the Supreme Being, ever-present in our hearts, guide us in our understanding and help us realize the Truth.

RM, Atlanta USA, November 14, 2021

Amma's love

A real Master teaches you to accept everything that happens in life. He helps you to be thankful for both good and bad, right and wrong, enemy and friend, those who harm you and those who help you, those who cage you and those who release you from the cage. The Master helps you forget about the dark past and the bright future full of a thousand promises. He helps you live life in the present moment with all its fullness. He lets you know that the whole of nature - everything, everybody, even your enemy is helping you evolve and attain perfection. -Amma

Mahatmas like Mata Amritanandamayi Devi, known to the world as Amma, are the pearls of eternal wisdom. Amma is the Avatar of this time. Amma's path is the union of Self with eternal wisdom.

All of Amma's actions point to that Truth, where everyone who walks to her gets enthralled with devotion. Amma has a multitude of tasks ahead which she accomplishes with ease. Amma Guides the aspirants who are passionate about the Truth. Amma's signature is love and compassion; as Amma says, 'I am love.' In that river of love, whoever takes a dip and sip a drop of love becomes that love. So the importance of serving the needy should be our priority, says Amma. The way Amma shows her concern and consoles those who rest their burden on her shoulders is incredible. Thus Amma, through her touch, looks, and words of wisdom fill hope into their lives. Thus they get the strength to carry their mundane life free of conflicts.

In turn, they develop the attitude of devotion and selfless service. This brings one-pointedness and purity to their minds.

Amma says an undisturbed mind is needed for meditation and selfless service helps in that process. For one's spiritual progress and for world peace, meditation is a must. Thus all Amma's activities and prayers are for world peace and harmony. The need to uplift the downtrodden and spread the fragrance of love is what is necessary to create balance in nature is what Amma conveys in her actions.

Amma says we need food for our body and Dharma Bodha (righteous attitude) for our welfare in society. Therefore, all wishes should be fulfilled in the light of a righteous attitude. Then share what we accumulate as equity to others through our actions. Amma says this righteous attitude gives way to awareness and discernment where aspirants will be ready to gain the highest Truth.

Amma, therefore, says 'I' and 'mine' give rise to ego where one loses self-control. Hence we have to see the error in that wrong understanding and realize the Truth by practicing karma yoga with equanimity in mind. The equanimity gives a clear mind to appreciate the Self through knowledge.

- **Swami Amritachitswarūpananda Puri**

Introduction

When you correct your inner vision through spiritual practices, the already waiting light of pure knowledge will dawn from within. - Amma

The content in this book initially started as a series of letters to my sisters of premonsatic life. They were curious about my spiritual journey and would ask me what I am contemplating and how to know the Truth in a simple way—so I sent them write-ups on various topics and a few as poems.

The topics and the discussions are mostly based on the wisdom of Amma, the Śruti Mata (the mother of all scriptures). Swami Kaivalayananda, our Acharaya who teaches us Shankara Bhāshya (the commentaries of Sri Śankara on the Upanishads, Bhagavad Gita, and Brahma Sutras), has also influenced my understanding of the Truth. As Swamiji says 'Truth is natural and simple, why unnecessarily complicate it unnaturally with our intellect, so let us keep it as simple as it is.' So in my write-ups, I tried to follow that advice.

As my (pre-sanyasa) sisters were new to this line of thinking, I kept the write-ups simple and tried to make sure that they can practically apply the truths presented here in their spiritual practices. These write-ups were compiled, and some modifications were made to it, which has resulted in the present book form.

Then by Amma's Sankalpa, Raghu, and Arpitha from the United States edited and helped with the formatting.

Through Guru parampara (lineage of teachers), this knowledge is handed down to us through direct instruction from the Guru. I am sharing the same with aspirants interested in knowing the Truth, which is Sat, the Self.

Before one turns towards the spiritual path, the outward-facing mind is often found to experience much struggle in relating with the world. When one struggles from these troubles arising from one's body-mind-world complex, they seek relief from such suffering. Such a person wonders 'Why is this world created in this way? Is there a path that allows one to escape these pains? Why do I have to bear these blows from life? How can I free myself from this ocean of samsāra?' During such times, one turns to God and prays to find relief. This is not yet a spiritual pursuit, it is more of a business arrangement one has with God at this point.

At this point, one's relationship with God is similar to the relationship one has with an ATM machine. When we are short of cash, we go to an ATM to withdraw some money. Similarly, when one finds oneself in trouble, one goes to a temple and hopes to find relief. They make vows or promises to God, or make donations, and so on, expecting that these actions will be reciprocated with God fulfilling their desires or solving their problems.

The real spiritual path begins when one begins to question and seek deeper answers to the fundamental questions of life such as "Who am I? What drives samsāra? What determines the events that are to occur in one's life? What is death and what happens to one after they die? What is freedom? How do we free ourselves from suffering?" So such a person begins the inquiry into oneself and life, and this stage is called "Jignāsa," which means "the desire to know."

When this occurs, the person is able to start spiritual practices. Such a person approaches a Guru, gets initiated, starts performing sadhana like Japa, archana, serves the Guru or his activities, etc. He also embraces forgiveness and looks to develop qualities like compassion. At the same time, he strives to restrain his mind from getting drawn back into pursuing worldly pleasures and objects, by analyzing the defects of the objects of the world. This beginning phase, where a person is striving, where discrimination and dispassion starts to develop is the first stage. In this stage, the aspirant also experiences some wavering and often finds oneself falling back to old habits. So progress in the beginning proceeds with stops and starts.

As one proceeds further, the aspirant's ability to discriminate and detach from seeking fulfillment from the objects and experiences of the world develops further. One clearly sees the flaws inherent in the world, and their nature to cause suffering. The aspirant understands the transitory nature of all things, their very nature is to arrive, stay for a little while, and then pass away. He seeks to maintain evenness of mind and seeks to cause no harm to anyone. Spiritual practices like Japa, meditation, and so on continue in this stage.

Aspirants on the spiritual path often feel like progress is absent, or not noticeable despite their performing much sadhana. One is reminded here of the story of a man who fell into a river and was being dragged away by the current. The man began swimming against the current, and despite swimming for a long time, stayed in one place. There were some onlookers on the river bank who laughed at the man's efforts. However, a wise old man who was also watching said, "If he had not been swimming against the current all this time, he would have been carried away and drowned by now. His efforts have kept him in place. Now pull him out with a rope!"

In the third stage, due to the growth of understanding, one strives further. The spiritual practices begin to bear fruit at this stage and the aspirant finds joy from spiritual practices. At this stage, one also begins to practice the attitude of being the 'witness' and separate themselves from everything that is perceived. The aspirant discriminates and adopts the bhavana (attitude) "I am not all that I perceive, I am separate, I am the Self, ever free, ever pure, ever aware" and distances oneself from the issues that would have troubled him before. In this stage, the practices of Japa, meditation, and so on continue, along with the practice of the attitude of being the witness.

However, in all these three stages, one believes the world out 'there' to be real. These objects, issues, pleasures, and pains of the world, because they are believed to be real, could still trouble the aspirant. Due to the objects and experiences of the world are still considered real, the desire and aversion for these objects and experiences still remain. Progress is not yet complete, not yet at 100%.

How is one to arrive at this completeness?

Through the practice of the Shravana, Manana, and Nidi-dhyāsana (listening, reflection and contemplation) on the teachings of the Upanishads, and the Guru's pointing to the nature of the Self as being of the nature of Sat-chit-ananda, ever-present, ever pure, ever aware, ever free Self, and that this is the seeker's real nature (Tat Twam Asi). In this Self, there are no negative emotions, no samsāra, no sorrow. The Truth though is that the objects of the world exist only due to the existence of the "Sat" nature of the seer, the Self.

The issues that existed before might still remain, from a material perspective, but from this understanding of one's Self-nature, these cease binding one. The Self was ever complete, what was missing was the awareness of one's Self-nature. Through the pointing out instructions from the Guru, this ignorance was dispelled. At this point, there is no longer a spiritual practice that is performed, beyond resting in one's Self-nature.

Until this point is reached, because the body-mind-world complex was believed to be real, one suffered. Once this ignorance is dispelled based on the Guru's pointing to the Truth of the seeker's Self nature, through this understanding, there are no longer any issues from the body-mind-world complex that trouble one.

One may say, 'All this sounds nice, but what about all the issues in my life that currently trouble me? What happens to them?' It is important to clarify here that Self-realization is not going to result in dispelling all the issues in one's material existence. One should not approach Self-realization with a utility approach. The realization of Self is of the nature of clarification of one's Self-nature, and one does not gain anything anew as a result.

Before Self-realization, one incorrectly understood oneself to be the body-mind, and upon Self-realization, one corrects this incorrect understanding. The issues relating to the body-mind and the world need to be dealt with at their level, with a practical approach.

However, from another perspective, there is a significant shift in the nature of one's interactions with the body-mind and world after Self-realization. Until the body lasts, the Jivanmukta (one liberated while alive), knows that gain and loss, pleasure and pain will continue to arise and pass away. The suffering experienced by those who meet every such event with desire, aversion, fear, anticipation and anxiety no longer trouble the knower of the Self. The Self-realized being is free from regret regarding the past, and fear or anxiety regarding the future, and meets each event free of desire or aversion.

Thus, we are not to seek solutions to the problems of samsāra through Self-realization, but instead, we are to realize that the issues of the samsāra are completely unrelated to our true Self-nature. To believe that the issues of the body-mind-world complex are real, that they can be dispelled, fulfillment thus found, and to strive towards them, such a belief is called māya.

The aim of the writings is to help change our focus from a body-mind-world frame of reference to one based on the Truth.

Therefore the whole idea is presented from the standpoint of the Atma (Self).

To briefly summarize the chapters in the book:

The first five chapters are brought out as Volume 1 and chapters six through thirteen are presented in Volume 2.

The first chapter, 'Our True Home' attempts to bring home the point that we are really Brahman the Truth. We misidentify ourselves with the body-mind-world complex and fail to see it. To realize our true nature as the Infinite, ever-free Self, the knowledge-based approach with rational thinking is explained through various examples.

The second chapter, 'The Door,' points out that the mind, its thoughts, sensations, perceptions, feelings are not our true nature. We are aware of the mind and its complexities. Therefore we are the aware-presence, witnessing Self. We have to clearly understand that we are the witness of the mind and its various modifications which are representations of the external world. Through the story of the traveler and the door, we discuss how the focus on the mind prevents us from seeing the ever-present Truth.

The third chapter discusses the various types of sadhana that are prerequisites to walking the path of Vedanta sadhana. In traditional Vedanta, this is called sadhana chatushtaya which include vivēka (discrimination), Vairāgya (detachment), sad-sampat (six qualities leading to one-pointedness and equanimity of mind), and mumukshatva (burning desire for freedom).

The fourth chapter deals with the importance of Shravana (hearing), Manana (reflection), and nididhyāsana (meditation) on Upanishadic Śruti's words. Like 'Thou art That,' 'This Self is Truth, Knowledge, Infinite, Immortal in nature,' 'Truth of the truth' 'Everything is Brahman,' 'Atma the Self is itself the Brahman,' 'I am Brahman,' and such Mahavākyas (Great utterances)

The Fifth chapter is about' Satguru.' It explains how Guru conveys the highest Truth of Self the Sat to disciple and touches on various aspects and the importance of Guru parampara (lineage).

Chapters six through thirteen are covered in Volume 2

It is hoped that the present work will be useful to the spiritual seekers in their spiritual quest.

Swami Amritachitswarūpananda Puri,
Amritapuri, Kerala

1

Our True Home

From that day onwards, I could not see differently.
I remembered that everything is my own ātma.
Having merged in the Goddess of all, I went forward,
renouncing all pleasure.
"Oh, man, merge in your Self!"
such principles that Mother told me
I proclaimed, wandering all over the world
in order to give refuge to sinners.

-Amma's mystical song, 'Ānanda Veethi',
The Path of Bliss.

This song from Amma attempts to describe her realization of herself as the Self of all. It was the moment of eternal bliss (Ananda); the moment of Her realization of the Universal Mother. From that moment onwards, Sudhamani became 'Amritanandamayi' (one who is full, filled with eternal bliss).

When She was Sudhamani, She was full of ecstasy. She was lost in Herself. But when She had the realization of the Divine Mother, She became 'Amrita,' the divine nectar that bestows eternity. She began to flow out of Herself for the benefit of mankind, in the form of Love and Compassion.

What is the nature of this Self, which Amma proclaims is our essential nature and exhorts us to merge into? Why does she begin every public talk reminding everyone that they are of the nature of Premaswarūpam (embodiment of love), Atmaswarūpam (embodiment of the Self)? Let us enquire and seek to understand the nature of this Self.

Truth

"There is One Truth that shines through all of creation. God is the pure consciousness that dwells in everything." - Amma

यत्साक्षादपरोक्षाद्ब्रह्मा य आत्मा सर्वान्तरः।

Yatsākṣādaparokṣād brahmā, ya ātmā sarvāntaraḥ
- Brihadaranyaka Up 3.4.1

Brahman that is immediate and direct—
the Self that is within all.

बहिरन्तश्च भूतानामचरं चरमेव च ।
सूक्ष्मत्वात्तदविज्ञेयं दूरस्थं चान्तिके च तत् ॥

bahirantaśca bhūtānāmacaram carameva ca
sūkṣmatvāt tad avijñeyam dūrastham cāntike ca tat
- Bhagavad Gita 13.16

The Supreme Truth exists outside and inside of all living beings, the moving and the non-moving. Because He is subtle, He is beyond the power of the material senses to see or to know. Although far, far away, He is also near to all.

Take anything that you perceive, like the objects around, which you can see, touch, smell or hear. Since one always assumes the body-mind-intellect to be 'me' and the objects perceived to be 'not-me,' let us explore — what is the material which made 'me' as subject and 'not me' as an object? What exactly is it?

Is it separately two different things or one whole picture consisting of 'world as outside of me' and 'me as body, mind, senses, intellect?'

Or is it that they appear in one Consciousness?

Where Consciousness as the screen enlivens all pictures as 'me' and 'not me.'

What is it that enables all of these to appear? Whatever one wants to name it, there is a substratum, which is the pure existence for all the pictures to appear in. This is the light of pure Awareness and enables all 'knowing.' Knowledge to take place regarding all pictures as 'me' and 'not me.' That means it is the very source- the Self, which is ever free from all these appearances as 'me' and 'not me.' They come and go from time to time, which is revealed when colored with that effulgence of Reality!!

With this exploration, we begin to see clearly that the one Reality modulating as 'me' and 'not me' is one whole infinite Reality!

In every experience, Only the Self, which is the substratum, is seen. Whatever you see, in all of your experiences, what is seen foremost is light. This light enables us to perceive the objects. So likewise, in all experiences, it is the light of 'Self' that is experienced foremost. When we wake up from deep sleep, we say -' I slept well, I did not know anything,' we only knew the light of Atma(Self), not names and forms, But we do not realize this.

Silence

"The nature of our inner Self is peace and silence." -Amma

Imagine listening to a song that had no breaks. If there was the only sound, we would not have recognized it as sound. We were able to understand the music, only because before the sound, there existed silence. It is through silence, the sound is. Silence is the very substratum and true nature of sound. In silence, from time to time, the sound appears and subsides back into silence.

Likewise, suppose we enquire how we see and know all appearances, both in the form of subtle thoughts or the gross objects of the world. In both these cases, we have to go back to where all these came from. Before all these appearances and experiences, what was there was only Existence (Sat), which is 'is-ness' without any distinctions and differentiation, non-dual without any second.

To understand such a state, we have to compare our day-to-day experiences of the waking and dream states, with our experience of the state of deep sleep. Without considering our experience of deep sleep, we would not have known the existence free of all appearances, so it is the deep sleep state which is 'natural and intrinsic.'

This very natural state exists right now as the very substratum and consciousness effulgence nature of everything.

Since we have come from such a state, we can infer and know; otherwise, nobody can experience nirvikalpa (free of distinctions) or non-dual nature because when experience occurs, it becomes vikalpa (distinctions), so the only proof is deep sleep. (all our experiences start in vikalpa only).

Through inference, we are coming to realize our swarūpam (Self-nature) is pure existence without any distinctions and non- dual.

If there were no such state as deep sleep, we would not have known or recognized our Pāramarthika (Ultimate Truth) nature as nirvikalpa, non-dual.

'Before the waking state is there deep sleep state. From there, only the waking and dream states appear and cease back naturally.'

'Before the appearance of the pot, it was mud alone, so mud is the substratum and the nature of pot.'

'Before appearances of pictures, the screen alone existed, so the substratum and nature of all pictures are screens alone,' 'on-screen all pictures are seen along with time, but the screen is free of imagined time, imagined space, and imagined birth and death of characters.'

Before the appearance of a wave, it was water alone, so water is the substratum and nature of the wave. Due to wind, the presence of a wave arises. The wind is creating an apparent separation of water by giving a name and form as a wave. This apparent illusion of waves seems to take over the reality of water.

Likewise, in the absolute existence (Sat), arise all the illusionary, imagined appearances (Asat) and seem to take over the fact! This is due to ignorance regarding the reality which is ever free!

In reality, it is the same state we are in now as the very substratum and swarūpam of all appearances. From nirvikalpa, we are coming to 'as if' vikalpa.

That is why before all experiences, our actual state, which is Nitya (ever existent), Śhuddha (ever pure), Buddha (ever Aware), and Mukta (ever free), remains now also as the very nature and substratum of all appearances.

One's Self is unblemished

"Look within, observe the thoughts, and trace them back to their source. Always be convinced, 'I am the nature of Sat-chit-ananda (Being Awareness Bliss)." -Amma

The Self is free of all concepts. Yet, for some unknown reason, due to ignorance, one thinks he is an individual with a lot of responsibility and pressure.

One thinks he has to undergo this happiness and suffering endlessly.

Slowly this apparent individual created various beliefs to overcome all his sorrows and started to live in those beliefs.

With this limited thinking, he thought about God, heaven, hell, wrote many myths, and told many tales to make everyone believe it. All these limited ideas are like fairy tales, like in order to make children happy, we makeup a lot of myths and stories without any basis.

Likewise, these beliefs are told repeatedly and imposed on others.

All cults, caste, creed, religion are the outcome of this limited ignorant individual belief system. But the reality is entirely different.

The Upanishadic Rishis say that all of Karma and its theories are told only for the purification of one's heart and finally to bring to the understanding that One's Self, the Atma is eternal, Ever Free, and that's what one's Reality truly is. So they imparted 'Tat Twam Asi ' knowledge: One's Self is the supreme Awareness only.

The soul (Jiva) going from and coming to the body again is just made up to make one aware about 'what is right' and 'what is not right.' This makes people walk in the path of Dharma, so it is mainly for moral conduct that all 'do's and don'ts' are told. With this awareness, one will not hurt animals, plants, humans and keep the environment healthy.

Mind and its latent tendencies go from one body to another irrespective of plant or animal or human body.

The subtle body goes and comes like various pictures come and go on a screen. Awareness, the Atma, is the screen here, and multiple images are the play of the mind and tendencies which appear and cease. When the pot breaks, space will not go anywhere.

So likewise, when the body perishes, or the body comes, Awareness will neither go nor come to a body. It only seems like that for us because we have not been discriminated against, which is 'Truth' and 'not true.'

Atma means Awareness, which is Oneself.

So when we hear these Upanishad's words, we will come to know about our True Self, not our false identified Self, which is just a bundle of the body-mind complex.

When we say 'I,' or 'I am,' that is the signature of Atma, which is unblemished Awareness, but when we say 'I am this' or 'that,' then it becomes a signature of the false Self, false identity.

Thus Upanishads make us discriminate and make us realize the Truth, which is Our Real Self, unblemished by all worldly concepts.

Recognizing the Self

"The Paramatman (Supreme Self) is everywhere. It is not a distant entity. The Paramatman is truly 'nearer than the nearest.' Children, you may search for God everywhere, but He is closer to you than you could ever imagine. Shake off your identification with the body and, transcending it, wake up in Awareness; then you will realize that God is 'nearer than the nearest." -Amma

सर्वभूतस्थमात्मानं सर्वभूतानि चात्मनि ।

Sarva bhūtastham ātmānam sarvabhūtāni cātmani

- Bhagavad Gita 6.29

One established in Yoga perceives the Self in
all beings and all beings in the Self.

When we see space between two objects, space between two words, space between two thoughts, slowly, it is understood that space is what is always seen first, and then followed by objects, words, and thoughts. Hence, everything arises in space, exists in space, and finally merges in space. In the same way, it is obvious that a screen is a backdrop for all images, like all images that appear on a television screen or like the pixels seem as all images on a computer monitor.

The Self cannot appear as other than Awareness. It is the very nature of oneself. It is immediate. It is the One that is available in every thought, sensation, and perception. Within and without, all beings are made only of Awareness and are illuminated by Awareness. Thus, inevitably Awareness is one, which is unchanging. We can perceive It; otherwise, it would not have been possible. It is the very proof of I - the inner Self (Pratyagātma) -the indwelling Self whom everybody addresses concerning everything. Self is immediate, first and foremost; all the rest are indeed its variegated modifications. By seeing the undivided Awareness as the very backdrop, one will know that Awareness is enlivening everything. Revealing itself in waking and dream states various appearances, and in a deep sleep, 'it is as it is.'

In all our thoughts, sensations, perceptions, it is Awareness revealing Awareness. Therefore, everything arises, sustains, merges in Awareness, as One. However, unless the Śruti or the Guru points out this Truth, it is not recognized.

'Pot space' anecdote

"A mahatma constantly shows the way. Patiently he instructs you, not once or twice but a thousand times. But you have to take up the journey." -Amma

Space is often used as a pointer to the all-pervading Awareness from which all that is perceived rises, persists for some time and then returns to. In the Chandogya Upanishad -

अस्य लोकस्य का गतिरित्याकाश इति
होवाच सर्वाणि ह वा इमानि
भूतान्याकाशादेव समुत्पद्यन्त आकाशं

प्रत्यस्तं यन्त्याकाशो ह्येवैभ्यो
ज्यायानकाशः परायणम् ॥

asya lokasya kā gatirityākāśa iti hovāca sarvāṇi ha vā imāni
bhūtānyākāśādeva samutpadyanta ākāśam pratyastam
yantyākāśo hyevaibhyo jyāyānakāśaḥ parāyaṇam
- Chandogya Upanishad 1.9.1|

Silaka Sālāvatya asked Pravāhana, 'What is the end of this
earth?' Pravāhana said: 'Space, for everything that exists
arises from space and also goes back into space. Space
is superior to everything. Space is the highest goal.'

There is a great anecdote that uses space to illustrate the
nature of Awareness.

One day 'Guru space' came and saw 'pot space' who was crying due to its limitations then 'Guru space' took compassion and
told 'pot space' - 'O pot space you are the infinite space' shake
off your shackles and roar like a lion asserting your infinite
space nature.'

Thus, Pot space is pointed back to its essential nature as
infinite space:

Then Pot space said 'No, I am limited space!'

Guru space said 'No, you are not limited space!'

Pot space said 'I was born one day, the Potter created me,
and then I am going to die one fine day.'

'Guru space' told 'tat twam asi' 'you are that all-pervasive
space, not limited space,'

'You, the space in the pot you are the same as infinite space!'

'There is nothing you need to do to become infinite space-
'you are that ever free space already.'

'You are free of all limitations,' and there are no limitations.'

Pot space replied - 'no, I am ignorant,' 'I am miserable,' 'I am
happy,' 'all these feelings arise within me from time to time.'

'Guru space;' 'no, even if you think so, still you don't have ignorance, misery, happiness. You are infinite and free.'

Pot space then asked - 'then why am I feeling limitations.'

Guru space replied - 'due to ignorance and illusory nature, you superimpose the pot's limitations onto yourself and believe you have ignorance and suffering.'

Pot space persisted - 'then why am I suffering?'

Guru space again patiently replied - 'there is no suffering in you. No attributes of pot can make you suffer. You are free of all limitations of attributes,' 'at the same time you think you have ignorance, happiness, misery while you have discrimination,' 'this discrimination that you are ever free is your real nature.'

'There is no real ignorance, and that is why it is only illusive ignorance and make-believe,'

'Ignorance is that which is only illusory and makes us believe in it. There is no real ignorance. Despite this truth, you are thinking about yourself to be limited. In reality, you are ever free, infinite, immortal, pure, unattached, awareness, bliss the Sat'.

Then, 'pot space' bowed down to the lotus feet of 'Guru space.'

Pointers to reality

"Know the reality"' -Amma.

You are the pointer!!

Everybody says, 'I.' That is the pointer to the Truth!!

'I' 'I' 'I!'

This 'I' is pure awareness.

Once it is mixed with body, mind, senses, intellect, it becomes EGO!

So wrong identification is EGO.

Once we become aware of this confusion, we come back to pure Awareness, which is our Self.

Withdrawing from wrong identification or recognizing this EGO brings you back home.

You as 'I' is the pointer to reality.

One is always doing Japa of reality itself in the so-called 'all things in the name of 'I.'

Without 'I,' nobody can do anything. So in all activities like seeing, hearing, smelling, touching, tasting, this pure awareness 'I' is shining.

This conviction in 'I' is realization!!

Reality of the world!

"You can understand the secret of bliss when you think of the nature of the Self. The waves of the mind will subside. Everything is there in you already. If there is faith, you can find it. The happiness that we get from the objects of the world is only an infinitesimal fraction of the bliss that we get from within." -Amma

Think about dreams,

There is no cause and effect.

No psychic power—all illusion!

This waking state is of the same nature as the dream!

The seer of dream and waking state is Turya is what is one's Self,

It is Turya spandana - Vibrations in Awareness - all this that is perceived.

Waking, Dream, Deep sleep,

That Turya you are,

You are that Turya,

The one who is listening to these Śruti words is the one who is Turya!

I.e., like Tat twam asi, he is That ever free Self!

Like one who is hearing,' you are the 10th man ' is the one whom it is addressed to, not someone else!

Upanishad says It directly in a simple manner.

We also should understand directly and in a simple way as Tat twam asi points to our real ever free nature.

By hearing the Upanishad, Know illusion as an illusion.

This is what the example of the snake perceived as a snake example refers to.

Instead, we give true nature to experience, which is actually an illusion (unreal),

Real is your Pāramarthika swarūpam the Inner Self

That when you are unaware of, you give reality to perceived experiences.

That Arivu(Awareness) is what is pointed here as you are Pāramarthika swarūpam. You, as Atma, are accurate.

Not as name and forms,

All names and forms should be negated; they will get negated in reality.

If you take all these current experiences in the waking state as accurate, what is the cause of this waking state?

You say the previous waking.

If I ask how the previous came, you say last, then endless previous will follow!

This is a logical fallacy!

Then if I ask -Which is the first waking state? First fate? First jiva? No answer. So there is no such first!

It is all nice to hear the word first, but there is no such thing. So it is called māya Anirvachanīya! Indescribable!

So, where is our world or creation beginning?

Chandogya Upanishad says, 'it is an Existence which is in all three periods.'

Not as a name or form.

As existence, the Awareness, we are eternal!

That is our true nature,

Not as this body, mind, intellect, world.

So it is an illusion like a snake,

There is no answer from where it came from.
But we are happy with the illusion.
From one illusion to another illusion, we move!
From one waking experience to another!
From one dream to another dream!
So in whatever way it appears in that manner, it is not real.
Our existence we superimpose on this and it feels real.

The effulgence of Existence and Awareness is seen in all experiences, but we mistake them as mere experiences.

It is light in your room expressing in each experience of the object, but we are not aware of light instead of the only object we see,
Switch off the light!
Do you see the object?
If it was present in whatever way it appears during light, then now also in darkness, we should have its experience!
Why, then, do we not have objects' experiences!
Because of its light existence, it's light effulgence which is seen through objects,
Not objects as such.

Similarly, now our body, mind, senses, intellect and the world are nothing but the effulgence of Existence and Awareness!
In deep sleep, we are one with Existence.
Now we see that Existence in all variety,
Never does Existence cease.
But names and forms cease in deep sleep.
So the truth is Existence.
We are That.
Tat twam asi (You are That)!

Conscious awakening

"May we all be able to light the inner lamp within ourselves and bring light to others as well. May everyone have the mental strength

to achieve this. May the grace of the Paramātma bless my children."
-Amma

As the rays are not separate from the sun,
We are not separate from the Atma.
Rays appear and cease, but the sun is unperturbed.
Names and forms come and go,
But Atma remains pristine.
Like how nature expresses its beauty,
In the Discriminative mind dawns the Truth,
As the screen is untainted with all pictures coming and going,
Atma is Ever Free of all agitation in the mind,
Like how bee takes nectar from various wild and poisonous
flowers and turns it into honey,
Similarly, all Life and death, pains and pleasures of waking
state become one in deep sleep as 'Sat.'
Through hearing about one's reality from the Sadguru,
One gets conviction when all doubts, ignorance get negated,
This Self-knowledge liberates from samsāra,
This brings contentment and fullness.

Light of Self

*"Children, we are the light of the divine. When innocence awakens in
our heart, allowing us to see everything in its light, there is only bliss."*
-Amma

In the light shines the light which is light always,
All the appearances seen in the light is made up of light only,
The light cannot be missed in any appearance,
The one who knows this light is light himself.

Mirror

"What do we identify ourselves with? If we enquire, then we come out of the confusion of superimposition." -Amma

In the mirror, the world of variety is seen,
In that mirror, all variety like the sun, stars, moon and earth exist,
But the medium in which they exist is one,
In the mirror, there is no variety as such.
So other than the mirror, there exists no variety of forms.

If we change our vision and look around, then we see variety in the world, but when we see the mirror, there is no variety, only one form, one medium.

So the variety that we see there is imagined, there is no variety, only one is present, only the one pure mirror is present, nothing else exists.

Then the variation that we see in the mirror as the sun, moon, trees, space, all these various forms are not what we see in distinct ways, but we are experiencing it. So without realness, for this reason, only we call it superimposition.

In the mirror, everything gets superimposed.
Their only reality is the mirror.

In the same way, these varieties of forms are inside, that means all these forms are present in oneself.

Why is it told in this way that they are present in oneself?

This body, mind, its inner nature, which is Existence, Awareness, Bliss, is all illumination of knowledge only.

In Awareness, a variety of forms are present.

Like how in the mirror (inside the mirror is what we say), not as real we experience variety.

We experience a variety of forms inside the mirror without any reality.

That we can understand, realize quickly.

As not real, we experience variety.

We are experiencing, but that does not mean they are real.

In the same way, internally, for the knower of Truth, all these shine.

Externally when we see variety, the ignorant feel it as real. Why?

Because ignorance sees all these varieties externally, even though not external, it seems external.

So for the ignorant, it is not 'as if' external. Instead, it is external only.

That means outside the mirror, what we see is real only. Their variety of forms are present. Between one thing and the other, differences are present. Still, if one can experience inwardly, that is from a reality standpoint. It is the effulgence of Awareness, which is illuminating all the variety, then the experience is 'as if external.'

Even though in reality, he experiences 'as if externally,' it is only within.

Like Dreams.

In the dream, we also experience everything externally only. Still, it is within

Similarly, all waking experiences are like a dream.

When we understand the Truth, then we realize it was all 'as if external,' not actually external.

Who am I?

"Look within, observe the thoughts, and trace them back to their source. Always be convinced, 'I am the nature of Sat-chit-ananda (pure being awareness-bliss)." -Amma

We service and keep the car in good condition, but we won't say I am a car.'

Likewise, keeping the body, mind, intellect, senses in good condition, and fit to function, but we cannot say I am the body, I am mind, I am intellect, I am Prana, I am senses because they have their nature and function according to that nature.

For example, fire burns, gives light, and appears splendid, but we don't say 'I am a fire' because our nature is not fire, obviously. Instead, our nature is free of fire and other worldly objects.

Likewise, the body's nature is birth and to grow into various stages from childhood to old age and to finally perish. In between it can become tall or short, fat or thin sometimes it gets disease so, keeping fit with good yoga, giving medicine time to time as required, is suitable for healthy living but that does not mean we can say 'I am the body', as it is not one's real nature, since the body has its nature it functions till it dies. Hence, our identification is only a misnomer.

The nature of the mind is to think either constructively or destructively. Sometimes it is sad, happy, proud, angry, etc. we cannot change this essential nature. It can be made fit and healthy by practicing non-doership, non-enjoyership, humbleness, free from greed, non-violence in thought, word and deed, straightforwardness, etc. But we cannot say 'I am mind' and 'I am those thoughts which arise in mind' because they are not our real nature, that which is not my nature, how can one say it's my nature ex. The quality of water is cool, so we cannot say it is my nature. The nature of each element respectively has its nature, so one cannot say it is my nature.

The nature of intellect is always discrimination. We can use it for the right purposes, but it is not one's real nature. Likewise, Prāna's nature or vital forces are hunger and thirst, so giving good food and water is ok. Still, one cannot say it is one's real nature by identifying with hunger and thirst and saying 'I am hungry' and 'I am thirsty.' Each sense has its function, and accordingly, it acts so do whatever necessary when they are diseased by treating and taking care of them but don't get identify with them and say 'I am sense' and tell whatever affects them such as blindness, deafness, etc. as 'I am blind, I am deaf, my eyes are troubling, my nose is bleeding' as it not one's true nature.

Identifying with the world, one says 'mine' 'not mine' that is also an error by superimposing ones nature in them, and there's nature in oneself and suffer endlessly 'I am lost' when he loses family, failure in business or become happy when one gains property, have a right family by identifying.

Then thinking time and space as ever-present one create permanence in the world by saying from time immemorial all these are existing and believing and thinking sentience is there in the society which is why oneself and all creatures are alive, this make-belief creates one to search for happiness in objects not knowing the world is non-sentience, impermanence, devoid of joy in nature.

Then 'who am I?' What is the nature of this superimposition? When this inquiry starts, it says about ignorance regarding oneself, which is the beginning and end of a Self eclipse.

'I am free of all nature of elements, objects of perceptions, etc., and self-identity with body, mind, senses, intellect, Prana, and world as mine and not mine,

I am existence wherein appear and cease the states such as waking, dream, and deep sleep.'

'I am the Awareness in which all activities of body, mind, senses, intellect, and world are known,'

'I am full, immortal, infinite, unblemished, ever effulgence, ever free, ever blissful Self.'

Who am I? 2

"We have a treasure within us that we will never lose, and that no one can steal. But we will not get it by searching outside. We have to look inside. We have to offer the flower of our heart to the Lord." -Amma

One is trying to search for oneself in many things by seeing oneself and recognizing oneself in others like children, husband, wife, and various relationships by giving multiple labels to them and concerning them. So one gets multiple labels and believes it is oneself. These labels or titles one tries to acquire in various ways for the sake of living is not wrong, as it is essential.

But to believe in it as oneself, not knowing it just as a role, is where confusion and conflicts begin within, as this process is endless. Every time things change, relationships change. One's labels or self-identifications also change. Thus, one's beliefs regarding oneself also change, finally, not knowing who oneself is.

Therefore we search endlessly for 'who am I' without knowing our true nature. This belief about oneself as an individual with name, body, mind, intellect, senses and all their nature as oneself is misleading, because whatever happens to body, mind, senses, intellect, one thinks it is happening to oneself, thus there arises strong identity with the body-mind and their conditions and says 'I am born,' 'I am going to die,' 'I am happy,' 'I am misery' etc, without knowing it is body's nature to take birth finally die. It is the mind's nature to be happy or miserable.

All such identification is veiling oneself by not letting one know one's true nature.

In the world and himself, one is searching, without knowing that he is searching for 'ever effulgent Self,' which is one's true nature.

Here comes the teaching of Upanishads and say this experience, this identification is not real and proclaims one's true nature as the Aware Self, which is ever free of all identities, but because of this ignorance, one believes they are an individual.

For this Self-realization or Self-awareness, knowledge of one's true Self is needed.

The individual thinks he is born and going to die; meanwhile, happiness and suffering are inevitable. Reality is beyond concepts of bondage and this ignorance.

Upanishads say whether one knows or not 'One's Self is ever free Supreme Awareness (Brahman).'

Then why is knowledge about One's true nature necessary? We may ask -

Being unaware of this fact about oneself causes the need for experience. This right knowledge removes the ignorance about this truth.

Upanishads, Rishis say that Oneself is ever free, but the Individual feelings or experiences about oneself are contrary. One thinks he is born, he will die, 'I am happy' 'I am suffering.'

This feeling as an individual 'I am the body,' nobody taught him it is natural or since the time of birth. This has become inculcated, hence from time immemorial, one thinks that one is born and dies repeatedly.

On the other hand, the reality is that 'oneself is ever free,' but no understanding of it is there.

Knowledge about oneself is not like knowing external objects as it is 'the embodiment of one's very nature, which is the essence of absolute Truth.'

Contrary to nature, about oneself as body, etc., or unawareness about oneself is not like it will be ever-present because, through knowledge, it gets destroyed.

One is unaware of this ignorance and how it becomes a bondage, because this ignorance is there from birth itself. That is why one understands herself to be the body, etc., not knowing like this is like an illusionary eclipse.

One is not enquiring whether this is all illusion or truth; just the individual is going ahead with a multitude of experiences.

This whole experience of an individual believing to be oneself is called ignorance, and he may further think he was born before and died, now also he is born and going to die. This type of experience is there despite being 'the very nature of Mukthi (ever free).' That is why regarding these experiences here, Upanishads say it is not real.

Another experience negates this experience. But, on the other hand, even though knowledge is not denied, 'one's nature is ever free' as it is ever fact.

Since one does not understand this Truth, the need for Upanishad's knowledge arises to attain liberation, and thereby ignorance bondage gets removed.

'Thus, in the inquiry of 'Who am I,' Awareness as one's Self is realized, ever free and unblemished by all identification.

Who am I? 3

"Many people think spirituality is just, 'an outlook' or 'a way of life,' but spirituality is more than that. It is a deep inquiry into our true Self. Real gain comes from the Self alone. If you do so, peace will be gained. Only inquiry into the Self is of eternal value, and brings peace. We should know 'That' as the true bliss." - Amma

Atma means the nature of one who is doing this inquiry or the hearer of Śruti's words ' Tat twam asi.'

The seeker is the sought.

Keeping the Red Hibiscus flower near a crystal, the crystal looks red, but at the same time, the crystal is free of redness, not after removing the hibiscus flower. So when we are experiencing all these pain and pleasure, life and death as the jiva, at the same time, our Paramārthika (ultimate) nature is free of all these experiences- this is the knowledge, awareness. Rest everything is negligible.

The experience of redness in the crystal is subdued in knowing that the crystal is ever free, pure, and untainted.

So all our so-called experiences of jiva bhāva get subdued in the Paramarthika jñāna that our Self is pure, untainted by all experiences. This knowledge is all liberation.

Do not expect some change will happen externally.

So in understanding our real nature, all these jiva bhāva gets sublated means we know it is unreal, Asat, like mirages.

So we should not think this knowledge is after all our problems get solved, there is no such problem situation in the Waking state. So if at all one wants such freedom from issues, then we have that experience in a deep sleep, so understand that and realize in this waking state about our true nature, which is Atma swarūpam and realize that we are ever free.

Know that, and experiences will be there but not Paramārtham (not reality).

Even though it is not reality, experiences will still be there.

When one has this knowledge, he becomes free of doership and enjoyership.

ॐ

2

The Door

"Stop identifying with the world created by your mind, and a new world will open up before you." -Amma

A stranger was going to his village, walking in the afternoon heat. The scorching heat of the sun was unbearable. So he was searching for a place to rest. The stranger suddenly saw a beautiful place with gardens and fountains. He approached the place, wanting to go in. As he came closer, he found a door to go inside. He started knocking. But it did not open. He shouted, 'Is anybody there to open this door and let me in as the heat is too much outside?' No response came. He was very frustrated.

Slowly he calmed down and started praying for the door to open. Still, the door did not open. He started meditating. But it did not open. He tried in every possible way to get help. But nothing happened.

After some time, an old man came out from the other side. The old man asked this stranger why he was howling. The stranger explained everything and lamented that nobody came to open the door.

The old man asked, 'How strange! Why didn't you see that all other sides were open and the door is just out there without any walls around?' The stranger couldn't believe how he missed noticing that! The old man said, 'You are so obsessed with the door that you missed to see that all sides were open.' Initially, the stranger said, 'I don't believe you.' Finally, the old man took pity and explained 'You were so obsessed with the idea that you need to open a door to go inside, and missed the infinite possibilities that were available to you. Similarly, we often get stuck in our single point of view which is like this door and such narrow vision simply deceives us.'

The stranger eventually saw the possibility which was right there in front of him and now felt surprised at how he missed such an obvious fact.

Then the old man said, 'The world does not change in any way nor does anything new happen here when you realize the Truth. Only the wrong notions that we developed from our childhood and the concepts that the whole world has embedded into us -- conditioning like our beliefs in specific cultures, religions and other similar beliefs -- these will be removed.

The old man took the time and answered all of the stranger's questions. Then, finally, in a very thankful way, the stranger enters the place by smiling at the door!

Hot summer represents this life, which is scorched with the heat of life and death.

The Stranger is the individual self. He is fed up with the way he is leading his life, and its suffering. Now he is lost, not knowing what to do. All his struggles, achievements, failures have made him very tired, sick, and scared. So he is looking for freedom from these constraints. He goes through philosophy books but is not satisfied.

He finds a place of hope. He goes there but sees the door, which is his ego (identification) blocking him.

The identification with the body, mind, senses, intellect, and world is the ego. Ego says, 'I' am an individual, born in a certain race, country, with a certain gender, having a certain family, belongings, belief system, etc. Now with this identification with all such labels regarding oneself, the aspirant starts knocking at the door -- but it does not open. All efforts to go 'beyond' and 'achieve freedom' only make one more strongly bound, as these efforts only strengthen the reality of the unreal ego.

When the old man appears - in the form of a Guru, with her infinite compassion, telling us "Why are you crying? Your real nature is infinity itself - 'tat twam asi,' You are That ever pure, ever aware, ever free Self. The Self unblemished by this ego, that is your real nature. Be aware of this fact and you are free! Stop believing in this imaginary world created by your conditioned mind and ego."

When the Guru instructs us thus, it is very difficult for our egos to accept. We refuse to acknowledge the infinite possibilities which are there right now in front of us. Instead, we chain ourselves with imaginary concepts and seek to find relief, chasing teachers, different yoga techniques, mantras and belief systems. Or we believe freedom is not to be found unless one gives up all their belongings and moves to an ashram or a cave in India or Nepal.

To be free, one needs to be first willing to listen to the guidance of the Guru, like the old man in the story helping the stranger who was dejected with his failed efforts. The Guru then helps the aspirant understand that in focusing on his ego and its seeking to 'achieve' something through the mind, he missed the simple Truth that nothing stops him, as all sides are open to walk into that place. Only his focus on the reality of the mind stood in the way.

The stranger did not believe this - so when the Truth is pointed to as being Infinite, Immortal, Eternal Awareness as our real nature, we don't believe it. So the Guru takes the special interest out of compassion and explains why we miss recognizing this Truth. Due to our obsession with our ego, we don't see that it is a great conjuror, which chains us with false concepts to a make-believe in the world and, throughout our life makes us think of the unreal as real and the real as unreal. Thus, we are unable to discriminate, even when the Guru or Upanishads point out our real nature.

The old man in the story said, 'you saw only the door, but not all other sides which are open!' Similarly, when we do all our worldly and spiritual actions through the ego, we will never become aware of the reality which the Guru is pointing out.

When Guru tells the truth about pure Self, 'Atma', the listener's mind should be available and the Guru's words should be heard with attention. This reveals knowledge about the pure Self by removing the obstructions in the disciple's mind such as 'I do not see the Atma, hence Atma is not there.' This means not knowing oneself as pure infinite Awareness and knowing one's 'Self' as body, mind and senses.' This recognition of the infinite Awareness which is free of all identifications, as our own nature has to be strengthened by the knowledge pointed out by the Guru that One's 'Self' is ever free. This brings the realization to the disciple that his/her 'Self' is ever free.

With thankfulness to the old man, the stranger entered the house and felt rested and refreshed. Similarly, with gratitude to the Guru and scriptures, the listener will realize his True nature of the pure 'Self' as ever free.

All experiences are of the mind

In the Bhagavad Gita, Sri Krishna says,

नासतो विद्यते भावो नाभावो विद्यते सत: ।

nāsato vidyate bhāvo nābhāvo vidyate sataḥ

- Bhagavad Gita 2:16

The Unreal has no real being,
and of the real there is no cessation.

So the ego is no more an obstacle, even when it appears, if it is seen as unreal. It remains but it is no more an obstacle. The 'Self' is free of the obstacle of the ego.

There are two aspects to the ego. One aspect of the ego is identification with the body, mind, and world as 'I' and 'mine.' The other aspect of ego is the seeking to expand our sense of 'I' and 'mine' through pride, possessions and so on.

Here we are explaining how to dis-identify with ego, the 'I' which identifies with a body-mind-world complex. Disidentifying ourselves from the ego is the way to final emancipation.

This is why Amma says one can be good at one's profession, or possess wealth, be skillful at various arts and so on, but while doing so, still be free of pride, arrogance, jealousy, etc.. What is needed here is to be free of likes and dislikes.

Ego in the form of pride, arrogance, etc., can be negated or taken care of by being compassionate, forgiving, etc., by cultivating and practicing good qualities. Through the 'thinning' of the ego by the cultivation of such virtues, purification of heart occurs and one comes to understand that the ego that identifies with body and world is unreal, and one's real nature is free of all these identification. We will discuss further on this topic of the purification of mind in the future chapters.

It is important for one not to get confused regarding final liberation or Moksha. The ego, which is imagined to be our true Self by ignorance, should be seen and understood as non-existent by focussing on the knowledge about our real nature. This is because ignorance is not something substantial to be destroyed; instead, it is only a lack of knowledge that gets rectified. That is the approach the Guru points out, to get rid of the unreal ego.

The Upanishads want us to see this Truth. There is no time involved in this. As soon as the guru points it out as 'tat twam asi,' 'Sat, you are,' it is realized at the same time. 'Sat I am' 'as our nature is ever free of body-mind-world complex identification and One's 'Self' is one with 'Supreme Self.'

All identification gets negated in this knowledge. Unreality has no being. We need not fight with an unreal appearance to make it disappear because all our efforts will make the unreal into a reality in itself, enabling it to survive and bring more suffering. That is why there is no place for such a fictional ego in our real nature. This understanding is all that is needed. This awareness is liberating.

The bloated ego in the form of pride, arrogance, etc is also a result of ignorance. This has to be removed through efforts, humility and selfless service to the Guru and by giving up the expectations regarding the fruits of one's actions. This creates mental purity and will help in understanding our real nature. Still, the primary issue we are discussing here is the misidentification of the 'I' with body-mind, and this will get subdued only by getting a conviction in our real nature and the nature of everything as 'Sat.' This knowledge is called 'Self-knowledge.'

Upon this realization, the world around us is still perceived in the same way by both those who have realized their Self-nature and by those who still identify with their body-mind complex. However, one who knows their real nature as 'Sat' pointed out by Upanishads and the Guru, is free of identification. Such a person sees the body-mind-world complex as the expressions of the Self, like water appearing as waves. We cannot expect any change in unreal appearances as they are only appearances by definition.

So whatever suffering one is experiencing will cease in this awareness that 'One's Real Self is Ever Free' of happiness and misery leading to fulfillment.

Ever-changing nature of the mind

"The mind and its thoughts are not real. They are the fiction of our own creation. Pure Awareness alone is real. Thinking may seem natural to you, but it is not natural. It is not part of your real existence. Your

thoughts and your ego create nothing but restlessness and agitation. They don't belong to you, and you will continue to be restless until they are eliminated." - Amma

We get carried away by the flow of our experiences so much that we cannot see the fact that the experiences, which are projected by the mind, are not our "Self," which is of the nature of pure Awareness.

We hold on to some experience and want that part of the experience to remain with us or as us for the rest of our life. But it is against the very nature of experience, because no matter what the experiences are, they have to change continuously to make place for newer experiences.

Most of the time, we either want a particular experience or would like to avoid another. But we forget that it is all one whole experience, and it cannot be divided into 'desirable' and 'undesirable' parts. Instead, we should understand that the experience's essential nature is that one part of the experience is followed behind by the other part.

This continuous flow of experience is what life is all about.

When we selectively want only the nice, pleasurable experience, a lot of resistance starts to build up. A lot of energy has to be expended to maintain a specific type of experience. It eventually becomes much tougher and tougher to support a particular experience. Finally, we get defeated in sustaining it. This situation leads to sorrow, depression, and despair. As a result, we feel we missed happiness in one way or another. It may even sometimes end in bitterness, rage, and a feeling of hostility towards the surroundings.

Both the situations – despair or rage - are harmful. We cannot always get what is wanted or avoid the unwanted. The fact of the matter is that all experiences flow through our body, mind, and whatever world we made for ourselves. They inevitably leave their impression of pain or pleasure, beauty or ugliness, gain or loss, heat or cold, like or dislike, etc. However, the essential point to note is how we relate to them or how we identify ourselves with them. That is where the difference between a knower of Truth and the ignorant one lies. The difference shows up in how the knower of reality and the ignorant one place themselves in relation to the ever-changing experiences.

Experience, as such, cannot create happiness or misery. It all depends on how we identify with the experience.

The nature of the body, mind, senses, intellect and the world will follow the way we identify ourselves. Hence, what matters most is where this identification begins and how we place ourselves with it.

The Self, as such, does not play a role in these. Why does the Self then appear to place itself in them when it is not its nature? Lack of awareness and ignorance about its essence is the cause of the mistaken identity.

This wisdom of Self is what the Upanishads and the Seers of the truth point out. They hold that the Self is 'ever free' from all experiences that the body, mind, senses, intellect, and the world.

When there is identification of Awareness with these adjuncts, it is the birth of 'the separate self.' Because of this confusion, we get caught up and spend the rest of our life saying that 'I am the body' 'I am the mind,' 'I am the intellect,' thinking and behaving as though I am a separate self, 'me' or 'not me.'

The world of experiences flows through this separate Self and whatever happens to the body, mind, senses, and the world around, one thinks it is happening to oneself and says, 'I am happy' 'I am miserable.'

This identity colors our experiences at all levels in the form of happiness and misery.

Withdrawing the Self from identifying with the body-mind-world complex is what wisdom is all about. In other words, it is called 'Self-realization' or 'freedom of the Self.'

Self is of the nature of Existence and Awareness, and thus It permeates all the experiences. Yet, It is free and flawless by anything like space. Space accommodates everything, and however, it is free of all the objects that exist within it.

The Self, which is ever free of samsāra (the ocean of transmigration), seems 'as if' it is experiencing samsāra in a waking state and somewhat in a dream state but free in the deep sleep state.

This awareness is necessary because we think that this modified world itself is real, and we take that whatever happens to our body-mind complex is all we are. Such limited feelings are felt in the dream state also. We think we are a separate self within the dream world, and we take it to be real at the time of experiencing the dream.

This belief reinforces the reality of the experience because we depend purely on the flow of experiences without analyzing whether the experiences like thoughts, perceptions, sensations, feelings are real, unreal, or illusory.

The flow of experiences can be anything; that is why we have to enquire into the nature of experiences.

Real or Sat 'existence' does not get sublated in all periods and states when all experiences happen within oneself.

A crystal does not get sublated, though it may appear red due to the redness of a flower kept near it. So likewise, the Self never gets denied despite the body-mind-world experiences taking place within It.

Just as the changes taking place in a wave do not affect the ocean, the variety of experiences taking place in a separate self does not modify the reality that is ever free of experiences.

The individual Self is just like a wave or an appearance within the ocean of Awareness.

Experiences like being frustrated about bondage or craving for freedom from bondage are the agony of an individual who is ignorant about their reality. It's like a child who feels concerned that his face is distorted or too fatty or thin-looking at the image of his face reflected in a mirror with uneven surfaces.

Whatever may be the number or variety of experiences, they do not affect the ever-free Aware Self, which is self-effulgent.

Ignorance arises because of a lack of discrimination. Discrimination is the ability to distinguish the real from the unreal. The reality is that there is nothing like bondage for the Self.

True freedom or liberation is ever established Self. Ignorance cannot exist once the reality of the Self is known.

'Sat' is only one without second, subtle, without attributes, all-pervasive, taintless, partless, ever conscious, ever free, ever pure, and blissful.

'Sat' is the substratum for all fleeting experiences which appear and disappear. It is independent and directly experienced.

Unreal or asat refers to that which exists during the time of experience but gets sublated once the reality is known. Experiences arise as a continuous flow on a substratum. Experiences cannot appear independently. They need a substratum for their appearance, like pots need clay, waves need water, ornaments need gold, and so on. The Self or 'Sat' is the substratum for all names and forms of experiences.

Some appearances are illusory, like mirages. Impressions won't return when reality is known as the snake on the rope or the silver in the nacre (mother of pearl). Some appearances do not exist at all, like sky flowers, rabbit horns, etc.

But as Sat is not non-existent like the horns of a rabbit, nor is it illusory. 'Sat' is one's own experience. It is the very first effulgence 'I.' 'I' is felt when we wake up in the morning from sleep. But very soon, we identify 'I,' the Self, with our body-mind-world complex. Our inquiry here brings discrimination. We become aware of our real nature.

Hearing the Śruti message 'tat twam asi,' one realizes Sat (the supreme Self) as one's real nature (Sad asmi-Sat I am), and all contrary experiences like that 'I am a limited self or individual' get sublated.

Just as the Sun never has known darkness at any point of time, understand that the Self never has ignorance in It and that It is ever free of all apparent limitations as body-mind-intellect.

Effort - contemplating the door

"Children, we are the light of the Divine - the eternally free, infinite and blissful Atman (True Self). Proceed with innocence, effort and faith and you will discover the bliss of the Self within you. Mother wants people to work hard in order to attain spiritual bliss. She does not want people to idle away their time in the name of spirituality. While people come to Mother for varied reasons, She will somehow make them remember God." -Amma

In general, there are three attitudes regarding oneself that are seen in the world.

The first attitude is when one takes oneself to be the body. Such a person believes 'I am the body,' and believes the mind exists within the body, and life begins with birth and ends with death. Such a person aims to accumulate as much pleasure, possessions and experiences during their lifespan and they fear old age and death. With such a belief, they suffer much as they resist the ever-changing nature of the body, mind and the world around them.

The second attitude is when one believes oneself to be the mind or a Jiva or the soul, which reincarnates. Most religions of the world preach along these lines. Such a person believes in the mind that reincarnates, and experiences the fruits of past Karma. These people, when they suffer through life's experiences, start treading the spiritual path and perform practices like charity, selfless service, Japa and meditation.

The third attitude is one where one knows oneself to be of the nature of Sat, the Self and as the Awareness that witnesses the ever-changing modifications of the body-mind-world complex. Those who are established in this are known as Self-realized beings, and those who practice abiding in such an attitude are those fortunate few who walk the path of Atma Vichara or Self-enquiry.

In the story above, the traveler who sat down and prayed to God and meditated in front of the door expecting the door to open as a result, can be compared to those spiritual aspirants who perform sadhana with the attitude that they are the jīva that transmigrates. They seek to create certain states of mind, like various levels of samādhi, or insist on always having certain kinds of thoughts and avoiding others. They also believe that through such practices, they can overcome suffering and the changing nature of the world.

When such aspirants fail to see results despite much effort, either through the result of past Karma or through the grace of God or Guru, they meet a realized being who through compassion imparts to them the Truth regarding the nature of their Self.

However, even when the Guru instructs us, we are blind to reality, deaf to what the teacher or Guru says. Then he only has to force us to hear the teaching and finally, one day sees the truth. Anything is possible by constant effort is the example set by the Guru.

The Guru is relentlessly patient and determined to make us understand. She wants to see us grow and become independent, as we are always used to dependency. She knows it is not helpful to just protect us, and often creates uncomfortable situations that promote our growth. Thus, the Guru creates conditions that enable our growth. The effort from our side is needed to realize the Truth ourselves.

Importance of spiritual practices

"Because our minds are not pure, there is a constant flow of thoughts unrelated to God or our true self. Purity of mind is the precondition for the realization of the Truth. Only through sadhana can we avoid being enslaved by circumstances. We should learn the spiritual principles by listening to satsangs, and then live according to those principles. When the mind becomes still through prolonged spiritual practices such as listening to satsangs, study of sacred books, selfless service and concentration, then it becomes possible to experience the ever-present hidden Truth." -Amma

A question may arise then regarding the place for spiritual practices aimed at purifying and creating one-pointedness of the mind. Thus it helps to discuss the nature of ignorance. The cosmic māya, which exists at an individual level as Avidvya (ignorance) has two effects. The first is called Vikṣepa (disturbance or distractions) and the second is called Āvarana (covering or veiling).

The constantly fluctuating nature of the mind is a result of Vikṣepa. With such a disturbed mind, we are unable to discover our Self-nature, and our minds remain ignorant despite the Guru pointing out to us the Truth regarding the nature of our Self. Thus, practices which are essential to purify one's heart can be performed. To name a few -

Selfless actions, with the attitude of not expecting the fruits of one's actions, or service to the Guru, or that the Self is not an agent. Keeping control of the body with exercise and giving necessary food.

Mind and senses can be made fit by restraining from unnecessary straying away from Self Practicing control of one's breath (Prānayama)

Developing good qualities like friendliness, compassion, equanimity and gladness.

Curbing desires, anger, pride, jealousy, to avoid aversion

Inculcating a good attitude in mind by chanting, by prayers to the creator, and Guru

The practice of non-lying, not-hurting, non-stealing, celibacy and simplicity in one's living habits

All of these help in developing mental purity and one-pointedness of mind. We will discuss the prerequisites to Vedanta sadhana in the next chapter.

With the calmness and quietude of mind that results from such practices, one should listen to the wisdom of Truth to negate ignorance regarding Self. Otherwise, just controlling the mind and being kind and doing good to others will not serve the purpose to realize the unreal nature of body, mind, and world and to end suffering.

We cannot change the ever-changing nature of the body-mind-world complex. We can only try to keep the body and mind fit by developing good qualities, and conduct ourselves so that we don't disturb society. We can also act in a manner that is beneficial to others, that is not the end of the journey. It is important to be aware that anytime one's mind can swing back to entertaining different disturbing thoughts and moods, which can occur due to a variety of reasons. The very nature of the mind is to facilitate the flow of constructive and destructive thoughts. If we insist on having only certain kinds of thoughts, we may fail in our efforts and feel depressed.

When oneself is imparted in the teaching 'thou art that' or 'your real nature is that Sat (Being)' then cessation of all our actions,

If spiritual practices are performed without understanding the ever-changing nature of the body, mind and world, it is similar to compressing a spring with our finger. When we let go of our finger, then it returns to its original state in full force. This is because of our belief in the reality of the body-mind-world, which creates resistance, and we try to suppress or forcefully contain.

In this process, we forget to know that the nature of the body, mind, intellect, senses, and world have their own nature and they will not change their prescribed course according to our imaginations, desires, fears and concepts. Without knowing their nature, trying to change or stop their nature through various practices or methods is all a part of ignorance itself. Temporarily they can provide some comfort or peace, but soon they swing back like a pendulum of the clock to the original state of mind with all its fears, anxiety and unhappiness.

This happens because there is a lack of understanding on our parts that misery and happiness will always exist as it is all part-and-parcel of the body-mind complex. When one takes birth, the human body is a result of the mixture of merits and demerits done in past births, which exist in the body-mind as latent impressions. The purpose of the human body-mind is to experience the result of the fruition of these past impressions. Depending on the latent impressions, sometimes happiness or sometimes misery is experienced and in between these swings, life flows with numerous experiences.

This whole life is a process in an individual with all sorts of twists and turns, which is called samsāra. It is the process of repeated birth and death cycle because again, new impressions create actions which are performed during the present birth. Hence this process continues as all the results of the actions are decided by the creator. Creator is the omnipresent, omnipotent, omniscient 'Sat' who created all the beings and by keeping rules or dharma or the code of conduct. Anyone who violates these rules reaps the results of demerits in the form of misery. Anyone who follows or respects the rules will be reaping the results of merits in the form of happiness and prosperity.

However, all of these occur in this realm of samsāra only. The sages who traversed the path of freedom from samsāra have imparted their wisdom to us through the Upanishads which proclaim 'you are Sat,' 'you are ever-free from this vicious circle of birth and death, free from merits and demerits actions, realize this Truth and become free.' Hearing these words with a quiet mind, one realizes 'I am Sat.'

So, to realize this Truth, the main job of the spiritual seeker is to become available to listen to these words. One's aspiration to know the Truth should be sincere. All practices of mind and body should lead one to hear these Truths and to get conviction in the reality 'Sat' which is 'ever Free of samsāra.' Then only realizes 'I am free of samsāra.'

That Awareness which exists in all three periods (past, present, future) and in all three states (deep sleep, waking, dream) is the reality of one's Self, free of doer-ship and enjoyer-ship. One's true nature is 'Sat' which is 'ever pure' ever free' immortal, unblemished, ever existent and the 'isness' of everything, awareness, bliss, one without a second, etc., This knowledge sublates ignorance that one is bound. All experiences such as 'I am samsāra' 'I am misery' this delusion gets negated. 'Sat' is realized.

Then the body-mind which was born due to the momentum from previous actions will continue till it falls off. For those who realize their Self-nature, their minds are steady with wisdom, and until the fall of the body, they respond to whatever experiences arise with equanimity, with the full awareness of their non-doership. In 'Sat,' there is no misery or samsāra. This is freedom.

Mind not your real nature

"Relaxation is the technique of witnessing your negative thoughts and the hurt feelings of the mind. Once you learn this technique you understand that the negativity belongs to the mind and not to your inner Self, your true being" - Amma

The mind's nature is to constantly change. A pleasant state of mind can quickly change to an unpleasant one, or vice versa, based on various triggers. This is what we always see in the world. Labeling the world and its objects or experiences as good or bad, pleasant or unpleasant are all subjective and dependent on the gunas (mixture of the qualities of sattva, rajas and tamas) of the mind. Much of the effort one makes, either as a pleasure seeker in the world, or as a spiritual aspirant who only hopes to have pure thoughts is aimed to keep the mind in a certain desired state, which often fails because of its ever-changing nature. However, through spiritual practices like Japa, chanting, meditation, satsangs (association with the holy) and mixing with Guru, one can overcome negative tendencies or bad thoughts which were overpowering us before, to some extent. These practices increase the level of sattva (purity) of the mind. When the mind is kept satvik (pure) through spiritual practices and regulation of food, activity and sleep, the negative samskāras (tendencies) of the mind remain dormant, but they cannot show up as satva is at the forefront. There is still a chance for it to get disturbed or to lose discrimination by Prarabdha (past life actions which gave this present birth), then one may lose control. This happens when certain powerful samskāras arise in the mind and seemingly compel one to act in ways that hurt one's progress on the spiritual path. Overall, it is important to realize that the mind cannot always be in one Guna; its nature is always changing.

It is also helpful to understand the mechanism of the mind. Vedanta divides the mind into four functions - Manas, Chitta, Buddhi and Ahamkāra.

Ahamkāra is the individual ego. Chitta is the memory and the storehouse of samskāras or tendencies, of which the vasanas are the strong likes and dislikes.

Manas is the part of the mind that processes sensory input, as well as brings up thoughts from memory, it is of the nature of sankalpa-vikalpa (conviction and doubt). This means, when an input is received, either sensory or a thought from memory, it seeks to question whether this particular sensation or thought is desirable or undesirable.

Buddhi is the decision making faculty of the mind.

When the buddhi is backed by the individual ego, the aham-kāra, all decisions are based on one's likes and dislikes, which are stored in the chitta, or memory. Again, these likes and dislikes also are expressed differently based on the predominant Guna (quality of sattva, tamas or rajas).

Self-realization, thus is the correction of the incorrect understanding of the buddhi, which looks at the Ahamkāra, the sense of "I" as a limited individual. When this is corrected with the proper understanding that "I" of the nature of pure Awareness, then the buddhi expresses the nature of the Self, and responds to all thoughts, sensations and events of the world free of the habitual likes and dislikes. Thus in the Katha Upanishad it is proclaimed -

एष सर्वेषु भूतेषु गूढोऽऽत्मा न प्रकाशते ।
दृश्यते त्वग्रयया बुद्ध्या सूक्ष्मया सूक्ष्मदर्शिभिः ॥ १२ ॥

eṣa sarveṣu bhūteṣu gūḍhosstmā na prakāśate |
dṛśyate tvagryayā buddhyā sūkṣmayā sūkṣmadarśibhiḥ ||
- Katha Upanishad 1.3.12

This Ātman (Self), hidden in all beings, does
not shine forth; but It is seen by subtle seers
through keen and subtle understanding.

So the subtle understanding, the conviction that the mind
is not my nature, and my essential nature is free of likes and
dislikes. This conviction in the upanishadic declaration of 'Tat
twam asi' 'Tat' is that supreme Awareness, that Sat (Being)
is what 'twam' you are, 'Sat you are,' this conviction is what
liberates. This freedom is not a state of mind, but a freedom
from the mind.

Myth and reality

*"There is no difference between the Creator and creation, just as there
is no difference between the ocean and its waves." -Amma.*

From a reality standpoint, creation is not separate from 'Sat',
it is only 'as if.' Only one 'Sat' (Truth, Existence) exists, that is
Brahman. In other words, the transcendental state of turiya,
also known as Pure Awareness or Self or 'I,' that is the true
nature of oneself and everything. That is why Upanishads say
'Tat twam asi,' that 'Sat' you are and 'Ekam Advitīyam Brahma'
which means 'Brahman is one without a second.'

Just like how we cannot separate water from the waves, or
cannot separate an image from the stone, similarly, from the
standpoint of reality, the creation, creator and the individual
who is doing this inquiry are indeed inseparable from the very
'Sat' the Existence, Awareness. This reality is the substratum of
everything. All else are mere negligible myths.

The negligible clouds seem to cover the ever luminous sun
by being an obstruction between the viewer and the sun. In
the same way, the negligible doubts seem to obstruct between
the one who is doing this inquiry and the reality 'Sat.' Through
enquire and discrimination these doubts should be dispelled.

Like how the wind dispels the clouds, enquiring regarding 'Sat' eliminates all doubts, giving rise to the conviction in 'Sat' as one's true nature.

Thorough knowledge of 'Sat', the veil covering the reality of oneself is unveiled revealing 'Sat' as one's nature. This is like the flame of the candle becoming one with the Sun's effulgence. In the presence of the sun, there are no two lights, like a candle flame and the glow of the sun. It is one light. But due to obstruction or limiting factors like a candle, it appears as if there are two lights, but in reality, they are one when all the limiting factors are negated. There is only one light, whether it is light in fire or light in a lightbulb or light in stars or light in the eye. Similarly it is 'Sat' alone is modulating in all names and forms. But due to identification with the body-mind-world complex, it appears as if there are many names and forms, and people feel their separate individualities. In reality, it is one, whole, immortal Effulgence of 'Sat' is realized upon inquiry.

All our efforts to inquire about the creation are like asking 'where did the elephant created by a magician go? How did he create it?' And so on. How can anyone answer the where-abouts of the elephant which never existed. Similarly, when we start to ask about the creation thinking it is existing independently, then all our efforts will fail because there is no separate reality to creation as such. All are appearances in 'Sat' only. It is 'Sat' alone there is no separate entity or creation, all are its modulations only. When we realize this reality, all inquiry regarding the world, the individual and the creator cease. Knowing that they do not exist in reality at any given point of time, is the permanent cessation of ignorance and the source of freedom, otherwise one still questions.

How did the world arise when 'Sat' is one and non-dual? This question should be cleared from one's own inquiry, not from another person's inquiry. The question is in the questioner, and the answer is in the one who replies. This is like trying to remove the darkness in one room by turning on the light in another room. That will not help in removing the darkness. The question will go in one direction, and the answer will go in another direction. That is why the answer should arise from within the questioner. Until then, the questions will continue to arise without any solution.

The game of life

"You own the entire universe. Throw away your begging bowl and look for the treasure hidden within you." — Amma

Freedom only exists internally, but we seek it externally and get tired or bored. Our Self-knowledge will not change external situations as they are tailored by Ishwara (God) according to our past actions.

We are in the game now, and both good and bad, pleasant and unpleasant are part of the game. Realizing so is all we can do; that is how we get into internal freedom free of the game. We do not understand the game's rules, which we are already helplessly a part of, whether we like it or not. All are part of it.

If you ask what the rules are, only the one who has developed this will know, so only Ishwara (God) knows

Nobody else can. Like a dream, we are not aware of the regulations. Yet we are in it.

But as the light of pure Awareness, one is ever free!

In that light, everything happens, like playing the whole game, but they cannot affect light, so one is free like light, free like space, that is why the one who is aware of himself as Satchidananda, without body-mind labels and is ever free!!

When shadows come, do not follow as they are not real.

All objects, body, mind, senses, intellect are shadows that try to obstruct the light, but they cannot because they are not how they seem to be!

Awareness is free, expressed in each and everything in all the states, by lending its existence.

All the time, it is peaceful. Now we are conscious reality free of the game, which may sometimes be severe games or sometimes cool.

Still, you are free of the game when it is pointed out, you become aware. Like in a deep sleep, you take some time off from play, but again you are back when you come to waking or dreaming.

Now through this awareness of reality, you are out of the game. The name of the game is prarabdha karma. The actions done in previous games will bring about this present one,

So this is one whole game where stages include past, current and future now the present.

It is like when the fire is burning the house, we have to first get out of the house, it is a waste to ask who lit the fire, how it started, all those questions will not help.

This game of life has taken wild twists and turns, now if we ask 'who is Ishwara? Where is He? Why has he done this to us or why has he created this game?' All these questions are a waste of time and energy to search for him or praise him or scold him or to find out the reason for this game being staged now.

Wise ones say first become free of this game as He, the Ishwara is only instructing through Vedas the Upanishads wisdom, which is pointing us to our true nature. This is Satchidananda. Know this and come out of this game.

So why can't we save ourselves listening to those precious liberating words instead of brooding over the game in which we are playing? Sometimes suffering and sometimes laughing, because of actions previously performed in the game and lamenting about them unnecessarily saying 'why is my fate creating havoc!' All these lead to more difficult game situations! Realize this and come to a simple solution pointed out by Upanishads and become free!

Whenever you touch the Self, you become free of game,

So how frequently you identify as the Self is all your Sadhana,Then at one point, you realize you are not carried away in the Game; instead, remain as ever inexhaustible light of Awareness!

All confusion is only because of this ignorance regarding Truth. It costs dearly by causing unnecessary suffering!

How far is one picture from another on a screen? No distance at all, it only seems so in 3D pics. Still, they all appear on one screen. Similarly, in a dream, the whole dream is projected in the reality of consciousness, there is no manyness. It is only an illusory appearance, when pointed we become aware and out now! We are free of this illusion; likewise, time, space, and causation is an illusion.

In one light of Awareness, all appear as a motion picture with a lot of drama going on in each one's life. Boredom is also a part of the game, and you are out of it when you touch the light of pure aware Self when the Upanishads point it out.

In the darkness, we get lost, not in the light, no more games! Don't go into darkness, thinking you want to make it interesting!

Negate all wrong notions. That is how our real nature is pointed, not illusory nature!

The seer of boredom is the light, the seer of the whole game is Awareness Existence. Without that, we cannot get bored or experience the game either. See the trivial boredom Game in the light of Awareness. It just dissolves. Then you remain as ever free light. As one, nature is an immortal light of Satchidananda.

Reflections

"We spend our entire lives trying to learn about the external world, yet we never try to learn about ourselves, the inner world." -Amma

All empirical transactions are based on the reality of the individual and world. We see many variations inside and outside of our minds, which gives us a spectrum of experiences.All these interactions are real in the sense that they draw our energy through perceptions, sensations, feelings.

You became a name, body, mind, senses, intellect and said this is me, all these are mine, those are not mine.

All these personal feelings are fictional, like a dream which has no reality of any kind. This is like one's fantasy, which has no basis. However, when we can recognize this fact in the light of awareness, there dawns understanding.

Human pity

"All of us are searching for eternal bliss, but we will not get it from perishable objects. How can anyone who is looking for happiness in the things of the world attain bliss that doesn't belong to this world?"
-Amma

When I was on a trek in the Himalayas this time, I saw beautiful tiny flowers, small birds flying in the valley and wondered for whom or for whose sake they were living?

The valley is full of green trees, from big ones to small grass for whose sake are they living?

What are these mountains, lakes, and streams of nature for? Whose sake are they present?

Why does a Human being think it is for him?

What a foolish situation he has created for himself,

Why can't he fly? Why can't he give joy like nature?

Why does he shrink?

Why does he exist?

Is he missing the very depth of his being?

'O' alas, can anyone help him,

when birds sing, flowers blossom,

while whole nature is in rhythm,
Is there any greater ignorance than this Truth? Human pity...

In the fire of realization

In the far valley,
Nobody to appreciate, yet the birds sing,
Nobody to see the beauty, still the flowers blossom,
Nobody to care
Yet the mountains, stream and the whole valley is full of life far beyond the human mind,
What is it that drives this eloquence of nature?
Then in my heart, the love of Beingness and Knowingness became evident!
This was the only Truth that removed the barriers and realized the oneness with everything as existence and consciousness!

Look within

"Meditation is the technique that allows you to shut the doors and windows of the senses, so that you can look within and see your True Self." -Amma

This life with endless desires,
Like always running behind mirages and getting lost,
No time to think and listen to one's heart,
Finally, one enters a grave but only to return.
Like how one gets relief in a dark forest by seeing a tiny spark of light,
Likewise, one gets relief in life if he has an iota of vivēka,
Let that spark turn into illumination by taking refuge in Amma,
It is her every gesture and every word of wisdom that removes the ignorance in oneself.

Like when a wave settles, it remains as the ocean,
Similarly, when the ego is given up, one remains as 'Sat,'
Like how a child finds the ornament around its neck,
Only when the mother points at it,
Similarly, one realizes his 'Self,'
When Amma points out that 'Self' is immortal.
Endlessly for ages, man has been chasing pleasures,
Not knowing that pain follows it,
As happiness and misery are the results of ignorance,
Amma shows this mistaken identity clearly,
Realizing this one goes beyond.

ॐ

3

Preparation for Atma vichara

"Before you sow seeds you have to prepare the land, clearing it of grass and weeds. Otherwise it is difficult for the seeds to sprout. In the same way, we can experience Self-knowledge and enjoy the bliss of the Self only if we clear the mind of all external things and direct it towards God. In order to gain pure love and the highest form of bliss, one has to undergo purification. Purification is heating up the mind in order to remove all impurities, and this process inevitably involves pain." - Amma

Self-knowledge, according to Upanishads, means the knowledge of oneself as the absolute Brahman.

Since we are ignorant about our essential nature and of the nature of the world, we suffer. The Upanishads make us aware of the Truth, point us to our Self-nature through dictums such as 'Tat Tvam Asi' and also show us the path to walk in order to establish ourselves in this Truth. If one is qualified to hear these Truths, by preparing oneself through the practice of the prerequisites, then such a person immediately grasps the Truth, upon hearing the words of the Upanishads.

In the absence of such preparedness, the words of the Guru and the Upanishads either fail to create the desired effect, and these texts become mere play of words, just more information that now further adds concepts to an already disturbed mind. So in the Vedantic tradition, there is great emphasis on the purification of the mind and the ability to maintain equanimity and one-pointedness of mind, as a prerequisite for Self-enquiry.

The prerequisites are called 'Sadhana Chatushtāya,' the fourfold aids that prepare one for the path of Self-enquiry. These prerequisites are as follows:

Vivēka is discrimination. There are various aspects to this discrimination, as one matures on the path, but fundamentally, this refers to the discrimination between what is permanent and impermanent (nitya anitya vastu vivēka). For the Vedantic aspirant, upon reflection, one understands that the Self alone has existed, while everything around them has changed or passed away.

Vairāgya is detachment from seeking pleasure or fulfillment from objects, possessions and experiences, either here or hereafter (ihamutra-artha-phala-vairāgya). Discrimination and detachment go hand in hand. One understands that nothing lasts forever except the Self, and all objects and experiences fail to provide happiness and fulfillment, nor can they end the seeker's suffering forever. This understanding enables the seeker to stop chasing these fleeting objects and experiences of the world, providing the seeker with a sense of clarity and calmness, enabling one to focus on the Self.

Shad-Sampat is the sixfold treasure of virtues, whose aim is to create tranquility and one-pointedness of mind. These are as follows:

Sama: restraint of mind

Dama: restraint of senses: Moderation of five senses (restraint)

Titiksha: Endurance, Forbearance towards all pairs of opposites, like heat and cold, pain and pleasure, and so on.

Shraddha: Faith In the words of Guru and Upanishads

Uparati: stopping of worldly action with the spirit of renunciation, to ensure that senses restricted will not be tempted again

Samādhānam: maintaining tranquility.

Mumukshatvam is the burning desire to be free. This is extremely important. In the vivēkachudamańi, Sri Śankara mentions that when detachment and the burning desire for freedom are strong, the other prerequisites naturally follow. On the other hand, if detachment and the burning desire for liberation are mild, even though there is the appearance of discrimination and the tranquility of mind are mere appearances, like a mirage in the desert. So a strong yearning for freedom is a must, it is also what is commonly known as devotion in the path of Bhakti or devotion.

With the development of these qualities, which are necessary qualifications, the aspirant's mind gets purified and one-pointed. Such one-pointedness is essential for hearing the great wisdom of Upanishads follows.

One may have the doubt that if one was firm in one's detachment to the world, and has equanimity of mind and so on, is this not sufficient for the cessation of suffering? The answer is that this is not enough, because despite all of these, one is still ignorant about his true nature. Self-knowledge or the realization about the nature of one's Self, and this Self as the Self of all, could still be missing. This knowledge is necessary for true freedom.

Imagine a precious jewel sitting on the floor of a riverbank. In the rainy season, with the gushing, muddy water, it is nearly impossible for someone to see that jewel. When the mud subsides and the flow of the water slows down, one is easily able to see and pick up the precious jewel. The sadhana chatushtaya is this purification and calming of the mind, enabling the inherent Awareness within to become apparent and immediately graspable when pointed out by the Guru and/or the Upanishads.

Discrimination 1

"Children, bliss is our true nature, not sorrow. But something has happened to us where everything has been turned upside down. Happiness has become a 'strange' mood while sorrow is considered to be natural. Real bliss will be attained only when we can discriminate between the eternal and the non-eternal." -Amma

Life is all about relationships. Every single moment of our waking and dream states are spent in relating to one of these 3 entities - the body, the mind and the world. The world includes the man-made society, which includes one's family, friends, co-workers, etc and also the nature around us, like lakes, rivers, the weather, animals, trees and so on.

In relating to these entities, the individual ego continually receives impressions. Each of these impressions are then received by the intellect, the Buddhi, with a like or dislike decision, and the determination on how the situation represented needs to be responded to. This mechanism repeats endlessly until death.

Due to ignorance, the individual expects to find happiness from outside, and attempts to create situations and accumulate objects and people around oneself that are desirable. Since it is impossible to exert such control over the body, mind or the world, because of their ever-changing nature, such changes create suffering in the human ego and mind.

Again due to ignorance, humans try to remedy the suffering and make further changes in the body, mind and world, which results in further suffering and the cycle becomes relentless. To make things worse, right from childhood onwards, one's family, society, all sorts of education and entertainment are designed to re-enforce this erroneous belief that fulfillment and success are to be found outside oneself, in the objects and experiences of the world. This results in the humans crying out from the suffering experienced from their failures to achieve such happiness externally. Such a person wonders, 'Why do I have to bear these blows from life? How can I free myself?' During such times, one turns to God and prays to find relief. This is not yet a spiritual pursuit, it is more of a business arrangement one has with God at this point.

At this point, One's relationship with God is similar to the relationship one has with an ATM machine. When we are short of cash, we go to an ATM to withdraw some money. Similarly, when one is in trouble, they go to a temple and pray to find relief. They make vows or promises to God, or make donations, and so on, expecting that these actions will be reciprocated with God fulfilling their desires or solving their problems.

The spiritual path only begins when one becomes aware of his shortcomings, and understands the flaw in their approach of seeking fulfillment outside from objects, possessions and experiences. This is the dawn of discrimination.

Discrimination 2

"True wisdom is that which makes life simple and beautiful. The right understanding comes from proper discrimination." -Amma

Until the dawn of discrimination, one believed that happiness could be derived from achieving certain success in terms of wealth and possessions, by surrounding oneself with family, achieving a certain look, and so on. When these strategies fail, and through God's grace, one actually realizes that there is the possibility of a different approach, one starts to take steps on the path of liberation. This also requires the reevaluation of one's relationship with the objects and relationships currently active in their life.

Discrimination is the firm understanding of the unfulfilling, ever-changing nature of one's body, mind and its thoughts, feelings and emotions, along with the family, friends, positions and wealth that consist of one's world. In contrast to this, the real nature of one is the ever-free Self, Self-effulgent, which is real and beyond time.

Our real nature is not that of the individual ego. Thoughts, sensations, feelings are the clouds that come in between our real nature and make us feel we are separate individuals. When we try to find the cause for those thoughts, feelings, sensations, we can see that it is due to ignorance about our real nature. This ignorance continues until we are told about our ever-free Self, Self-effulgent, which is real and beyond time.

Discrimination 3

"It is up to us to choose between temporary happiness, which will culminate in never-ending suffering and unhappiness; or temporary pain which will culminate in everlasting peace." -Amma

The maturing of discrimination occurs over time. In the beginning, once one is convinced that the world cannot provide true happiness or fulfillment, they start walking the spiritual path and perform spiritual practices. Such a person approaches a Guru, gets initiated, starts performing sadhana like Japa, archana, serves the Guru or in his activities, etc. He strives to cultivate positive qualities like humility, forgiveness, compassion, being helpful to the needy, straightforwardness etc. At the same time, he strives to restrain his mind from getting drawn back into pursuing worldly pleasures and objects. This beginning phase, where a person is striving, yet often stumbles is the first stage. There is one important mistake aspirants usually make at this stage. They have made the mistake of identifying with the mind and taking the thoughts that pass through their mind as real. In striving to keep the mind 'spiritual,' they are fighting against the nature of the mind.

So the maturing of discrimination is also the realization of the transitory nature of the mind itself. The aspirant understands the transitory nature of all thoughts. Their very nature is to arrive, stay for a little while and then pass away. It is the play of gunas. With this, He seeks to maintain evenness of mind, as the witnessing Self. This is an extremely important shift in perspective which brings much progress and peace to the aspirant.

Discrimination 4

"Children, discrimination is meant for one who is in the process of evolution. You need strict discrimination to understand the difference between what is good for your spiritual progress and what will create obstacles in your path. A seeker must discriminate between what is eternal and what is non-eternal. But once you have attained the state of Perfection, you have renounced everything, even discrimination. You cannot hold onto anything. Transcending all dualities, you become the universe; you become expansiveness itself. You become both day and night. You go beyond purity and impurity." -Amma

To practice discrimination is to bring the understanding of the eternal, ever-free, ever aware nature of one's Self in relating to the changes in the body, mind's thoughts and emotions and to the world. Such a being watches the changes in the body-mind-world with the attitude of a witness and remains unaffected, without the desire to possess or to push away any situation. In practice, one also refrains from seeking pleasures or fulfillment from the world, and adjusts one's life and relationships such that they are not a distraction to the spiritual path.

One may ask what is the specialty of knowledge? Just knowing unreal as unreal, and knowing that the Self alone is real. How does it help?

When the Truth is known about the nature of one's Self, then all worldly experiences get dimmed and feel like a mirage. With the dawn of Self-knowledge, ignorance ceases. So, freedom or liberation means that the belief in the reality of the pain-pleasure nature of the body-mind-world complex is negated. These experiences continue, but one is firm in the understanding that pain and pleasure are unreal; in Me, no pain and pleasure exist.

Dispassion

"Vairāgya, or dispassion, is when we renounce worldly things, realizing, 'All the joy I get from outside of myself is transitory, and will later cause me suffering. The happiness I get from worldly objects isn't permanent; it is momentary and therefore unreal.' To experience real happiness, eternal peace and eternal bliss, we have to attain what is real, one has to go beyond the mind and its functions." - Amma

When people experience suffering, either in their daily lives and especially during times of loss, like during the recent COVID-19 situation, or when accidents, death, etc occur within the circle of one's family and friends, or due to losses in a business endeavor, people feel dejected and temporarily feel a kind of detachment or dispassion from the world. Usually, most people recover from such blows of life, shake off the detachment felt, and prod forward. This is called "smashāna Vairāgya" or "deceptive detachment" felt in a crematorium, or due to a significant loss. One could use such situations to reflect and deepen their detachment, but usually, people lack such an ability to enquire into what truly happened. Such thoughts again arise when more one receives more such blows from life.

One may also chase pleasures. It is not that there are no pleasures in the world, but they are transitory and keep one constantly chasing them. Often it seems like the pleasures are short, and the pains last much longer. So these blows of life and the disappointment from transitory pleasures may cause one to begin reflection on a path to free oneself. One begins to wonder "Why do I suffer so much? Is there a path to free myself from all this?" Such a nascent inquiry, this seeking of freedom from the turbulence of life, is called "Jigñasa," which means "the desire to know." Earlier, one had a "Jigñasa" regarding the world, but now, when the person understands that the world will not satisfy his or her needs for true happiness, they enquire into the spiritual path. This turning of the mind towards the spiritual path is a result of God's grace.

When such a desire to know dawns on an individual, a person begins to read books, listen to satsangs, go to ashrams, seek out gurus, and so on. So due to this, self-reflection or introspection begins. One may even begin to practice spiritual sadhana like charity, selfless service, Japa, meditation, etc. This dawning of discrimination and detachment, where a person starts making spiritual effort and to control their mind and senses is called "Yatamāna Vairāgya," which means "the force behind making an effort." In this stage, one is making an effort to free themselves from their mind's habitual tendency to seek pleasures from the world.

After progressing further, detachment develops into a stage called "Vyatirēka Vairāgya," which means "isolating one from another." During this stage, one has realized that the objects and pleasures of the world will not fully satisfy his or her desire for happiness. One realizes the objects and pleasures of the world are fleeting and in turn bring suffering. At this stage, the person also makes more effort in their sadhana. Yet, at times, a person in this stage could fall from this understanding and feel immersed in the world, and when that passes, returns to the sadhana.

In the third stage, called "Ekendriya Vairāgya" meaning "related to one sense," an aspirant has progressed much further, and possesses strong discrimination and detachment. In this stage, the person is able to separate themselves from not only the objects and pleasures of the world, but also are able to distinguish themselves from the thought waves that arise in their minds. They are able to take the position of the "witness" and discriminate that whatever they can perceive cannot bring them fulfillment. Their "lakshya bodha" meaning the 'awareness on the goal' is firm, and they have a firm desire to know the Truth regarding themselves, and thus they are able to use their discrimination to stay on the path.

However, in all these three stages, one believes the world out 'there' to be real. These objects, pleasures, pains of the world, because they are believed to be real, could still trouble the aspirant. The Truth though is that the objects of the world exist only due to the existence of the "Sat" nature of the seer, the Self. People usually chase the pleasures and objects of the world, taking them to be real, and believing that by attaining these, they would find happiness and fulfillment. The Truth, however, is that all objects exist due to a borrowed reality from the Self (Atma), and can add or remove nothing from the Self's nature of being complete in itself.

The Guru points to the nature of the Self as being of the nature of Sat-chit-ananda, ever-present, ever pure, ever conscious, ever free Self. In this Self, there are no negative emotions, no samsāra, no sorrow. Through identification, one believes all of these to be real and tries to free oneself from them. Take the state of deep sleep (sushupti), one exists alone, as pure awareness without any adjuncts like the world, the mind or the intellect. Due to our being unaware of this state of Awareness, which is complete, we take the world to be real. This is māya, which is anirvachanīya (indescribable).

This is the knowledge that is necessary, the knowledge of one's Self-nature. When one realizes thus, in the waking state, that there is no such independent reality as the "world," that it is borrowed from Self, this awareness sets one free. Such knowledge, this awareness destroys sorrow. The Upanishad proclaims "dvitēyād vai bhayam bhavati" which means "In duality alone does fear exist."

In sleep, since we had no recognition of the mind or the outside world, we have no problems. Our issues however exist in the waking state. Upon waking, if we can similarly negate duality, all problems become non-existant. Our Self-nature is currently obstructed by our perception of the body-mind-world complex as reality, like the sun or moon is obstructed from our view during an eclipse.

With the firm establishment of detachment from the seeking of fulfillment from the objects and pleasures of the world, and is established in Self-nature, it is called "Vaśikara Vairāgya," one could also call this state "jñāna" or "Self-knowledge." In this state, there is the absence of duality, and thus there is freedom from fear.

This knowledge was necessary because of the absence of right understanding. Once the right understanding is established, one gives up both knowledge and ignorance and rests in Self-nature. In childhood, the mother repeatedly teaches the child about itself. It teaches the child that it is a boy or a girl, and how to appropriately act based on gender. In case the child gets confused, the mother again reminds the child regarding its gender and appropriate behavior based on its gender. Once this knowledge gets confirmed, now the child is conditioned, loses its gender confusion and acts accordingly. Similarly, knowledge was necessary here, to remind oneself of their nature as Sat-Chit-Ananda, through repeated Shravana, Manana and nididhyāsana (listening, reflection and contemplation), once one is established in their Self-nature, there is no need for further need for such practice either. In the example of the tenth man, pointing to the tenth man as the missing person was required until there was doubt. Once that confusion is removed, and the tenth man realizes himself to be the missing person, there is no further need to repeatedly remind him. Thus, all doubts are resolved and one rests as the Self.

Shad-sampat

"Bliss is not obtained from exterior objects. It is experienced when the sense organs merge in the mind through meditation. Therefore, if you want bliss, try to acquire concentration." -Amma

As mentioned earlier, the Shad-sampat refers to the Six-fold virtues that are aimed at creating one-pointedness and tranquility of mind. One must not see all of these as separate. They are not six, separate practices. It is more like a garland of various gems threaded together, which mutually help each other in practice.

These six virtues are shama (restraint of mind), dama (restraint of senses), titiksha (endurance, forbearance), shraddha (faith), Uparati (curbing worldly activities) and Samādhānam (tranquility).

The mind is the primary tool one has at their disposal on the spiritual path. The goal through the cultivation of these sixfold virtues is to transform the ordinary, distracted mind into a sharp, one-pointed tranquil mind that can remain unaffected and undistracted by the pleasures and pains of the world.

In the Gita, Lord Krishna says:

बन्धुरात्माऽऽत्मनस्तस्य येनात्मैवात्मना जितः ।
अनात्मनस्तु शत्रुत्वे वर्तेतात्मैव शत्रुवत् ॥६:६॥

bandhurātmātmanastasya yenātmaivātmanā jitaḥ
anātmanas tu śatrutve vartetātmaiva śatru-vat
- Bhagavad Gita 6:6

For those who have conquered the mind, it is their friend. For those who have failed to do so, the mind works like an enemy.

It is important to note though that the one-pointedness obtained here is then to be directed towards Self-enquiry, without which true freedom cannot be obtained. When one's doubts regarding the Self are resolved and one rests as the Self. One no longer needs to practice stilling the mind to attain yoga samādhi. When one knows the unreality of the mind, the stillness or the movement of the mind becomes irrelevant. With Self-knowledge, one ceases to care about the state of the mind, or the gain and loss in the world, or regarding one's designation in life. There is no longer the compulsion to achieve some state of mind, even to claim things like "I have conquered lust," etc. Once one knows their nature, there is no longer the need to claim anything either regarding their state, they simply rest content in their Self-nature.

However, until such a state is achieved, the aspirant is to diligently continue the practice of discrimination, detachment, one-pointnesss of mind with a burning desire for freedom.

Shama and dama - mind and senses control

"Bliss is not obtained from exterior objects. It is experienced when the sense organs merge in the mind through meditation. Therefore, if you want bliss, try to acquire concentration." - Amma

Shama or restraint of the mind, is the practice of retaining the mind within, either with the support of an object like the mantra, or to focus on the Self. This is because when thoughts stray away from the Self, we go out in the world of objects.

Dama is the restraint of the senses. This means restraining the five senses of knowledge, which are the ears, skin, eyes, nose and tongue, and similarly the organs of action like hands, feet, vocal chords, reproduction and excretion. The senses naturally lean outward, and when they come in contact with sense objects, they pull the mind outward to the sense objects, which then cause the ripple effect of creating multiple other thought waves in the mind.

It is important to be clear about why such restraint is essential to progress on the spiritual path. Restraint is not to be confused with suppression or repression. Restraint is a channeling of energy toward the accomplishment of a desired outcome. The lakshya bodha, the awareness of the goal is key. For eg: If someone desired to lose weight, for health purposes, then they would curtail the amount of sugar intake, eat regularly, get exercise and so on, despite being around temptations or feeling lazy to exercise. It is again an example of making informed choices with the awareness of the desired goal. Mumukshatvam is similarly described as the burning desire for freedom or liberation. When the goal is desired with such intensity, then anything that takes away from it, anything that slows us down from achieving it, is curtailed. This is where Shama and Dama come in. They are preventing the leaking away of accumulated spiritual energy through the extroverted mind and senses.

If we see a mirror without an aluminum coat behind, then our vision passes through the glass. In the same way, when there is no restraint of senses, they flow outwards, and the mind also cannot be controlled. Therefore, the restraint of the mind and senses need to go hand in hand with helping each other for control.

Without mind control, one cannot control the senses; therefore, for dama, shama is required. At the same time, without restraining the senses from being in situations where they are naturally pulled outward, one cannot effectively restrain the mind. Moreover, without such mind and sense control, being immersed in the world of external objects such as woman, son, wealth, etc., will not enable shraddha in the words of Vedanta and Guru; therefore, such restraint also helps in the cultivation of Shraddha.

A good story to illustrate why simply restraining the senses and stopping worldly activity is not enough to control the mind is that of the pious cat which was raised in a holy environment. Even when the cat is raised by giving good milk, it will not keep quiet when it sees a rat, it will pounce on it. In the same way, when the mind achieves uparati from objects, it will somehow try to free the noose of control. Then, without stopping, it will pounce on whatever sense objects it gets, so for uparati and dama to be successful, the restraint of the mind is essential.

Paying attention

"First of all, external alertness and awareness is necessary. As long as you don't have this, it won't be possible for you to conquer your inner nature." - Amma

Amma uses the word Shraddha in a slightly different context from the Sanskrit meaning. When Amma says perform all actions with Shraddha, she's using the word in the South Indian context and it means to pay attention to whatever action one is performing. In other words, being mindful. This practice is an invaluable aid in the practice of restraining the mind and senses (Shama and Dama).

Developing the habit of performing all actions mindfully, with our focus on the task at hand, while inwardly chanting our mantra or maintaining awareness of the breath or the Self, becomes a form of meditation in action. While walking, practice being aware of each step, while inwardly focused on the mantra, etc. This is meditation in action. As this practice deepens, life becomes a continuous meditation and the line between sitting meditation and activity blurs.

Shraddha

"A person endowed with faith in the Supreme holds on to that principle when a crisis occurs. It is this faith, which gives him or her a strong and balanced mind to enable him or her to confront any trying situation."
- Amma

Shraddha or Faith refers to the trust one needs to have in the teachings of the scriptures and the Guru. Without this faith, there is little chance of progress. Without the belief that the efforts one makes will yield the desired results, what enables a person to keep striving? Even in learning something related to the world, like mathematics, or physics, we listen to the professor with the faith that they know something we do not, and that by practicing what they teach, we will find similar results. This trust enables one to persevere, even when they experience temporary failures. Similar is true on the spiritual path.

Shraddha is like a vessel for preparing curds; where the rest of the sadhana we perform is like curds. If the vessel is broken or not cleaned, all sadhana goes to waste. If shraddha exists, then all sadhana will be victorious. Shraddha is the essential component for the fruition of knowledge. That is why we should nurture our faith and protect it from bad influences.

So what is being highlighted here is that faith in the Guru and the teachings is necessary, but this does not mean we sit and wait to be saved, or to be rewarded with heaven or liberation because of our faith. Shraddha here is essentially the trust and willingness to follow the instructions of the scriptures and Guru and verify it ourselves. Amma says - "Both faith and effort are needed. If you plant a seed, it will sprout, but for it to grow properly, it needs water and fertilizer. Faith will make us aware of our true nature; but to experience it directly, we need to put forth the effort."

Uparati

"To attain real peace and true happiness one has to go beyond the mind and its desires. No matter how much you may try, it is not possible to taste the bliss of the Self while at the same time seeking worldly happiness. If you eat payasam (sweet rice pudding) from a vessel used for storing tamarind, how can you get the real taste of the payasam?"
-Amma

Uparati refers to the giving up of worldly activities which pull the mind and senses outwards, this creates favorable conditions for one's practice and avoids unwanted and avoidable distractions.

In order to practice and progress on the spiritual path, one need not renounce one's home and become a monk. Having come to understand that there is really no true happiness in this world, one starts walking the spiritual path. However great our achievements in this world may be, we understand that one does not find fulfillment in this world. But walking on the spiritual path does not mean coming to or living in an ashram. It is really about the spiritual enquiry within.

Our focus should really be on our true nature -' Who am I?' One can be a young student, or a householder doing her daily job, a sanyasi in an ashram, or a person leading a retired life. The stage of life or kind of job one is engaged in, matters little. The essential thing though is to adjust our life situation such that it does not interfere with our spiritual progress.

Spirituality is not about trying to live a poor life, or doing things like eating just rice gruel, sleeping on the floor, eating sparingly or wearing a certain type or color of clothes,etc. It is not just about practicing austerities or living a simple lifestyle. In the olden days, spiritual aspirants used to go to the forest or beg for food in villages. However those practices should not be our focus in the present times.

Spiritual aspirants today are very much in touch with society whether we live in an ashram or at home. Changing one's location has not changed the link with society. There is really no need to give up our jobs or other worldly responsibilities. Where we stay, what we eat, what we wear and so on is not an obstruction to our spiritual life, as long as we focus on our real internal nature, rather than on external aspects of life.

We need to earn an income to maintain a family or to practice charity like supporting an ashram through donations. So earning income through honest, truthful means is not wrong. Eating poorly, fasting, avoiding sleep or other physical hardships is not spirituality. Neither does eating healthy food with adequate amounts of protein and so on go against spirituality.

So what is uparati in the modern world? It is an adjustment of one's focus. Instead of focusing all of one's activities to achieve wealth, possessions, experiences in the outer world to find pleasure and avoid pain, one shifts to making their inner life the priority. No matter what our role is in the external world, we are to use it as the means to develop divine qualities and to realize our Self-nature, just like Arjuna, despite being a warrior on the battlefield, realized his Self-nature and achieved contentment.

Attitude in action

" Children experience the bliss that comes from one-pointed focus on God. If you perform your actions with awareness and compassion and with your mind surrendered to God, bliss will be yours forever. Then, even occasions that would normally be painful are transformed into moments of joy." - Amma

Even when performing such essential actions in the world, the aspirant further refines his actions by adjusting his attitudes. For most of us, we perform the majority of the actions with an attitude of doer-ship and enjoyer-ship. While living in the world, with all our senses influencing our attention towards the external objects, it is difficult to have this attitude of non-doer and non-enjoyers. Yet, through the suffering experienced in the world due to various unexpected events and experiences, upon some reflection, it is not difficult to realize that one has little control over the outcomes even when actions are performed to the best of our ability. In addition, often completely unexpected events surface and influence our lives. So a reflective person understands that in life, neither the outcomes of one's actions, nor the circumstances of one's life are fully under our control. The beginning of Karma yoga is the practice of these realizations in one's life and actions.

For the practice of Karma yoga, one should have a clear concept in his mind or imagine that he is not the doer nor the enjoyer. We should train at least a part of our mind to think in these lines, and the rest of the mind can continue with the usual routine. Gradually we will be able to increase that portion of the mind that has been trained to see that one is not the doer nor the enjoyer.

We may question, why do we have to train the mind to nurture such an attitude? This is because the nature of the mind is to try and fit everything into its mental concepts of likes and dislikes. So everything that does not agree with the existing mental conditioning causes stress, confusion and suffering. To begin with, we start by imagining or conceptualizing this attitude. As the dictum goes, 'Yad bhāvam tad bhavati'- 'whatever your attitude is, so you become.' We may ask why it is important to believe that one is not the doer nor the enjoyer? This is because our swarūpa or nature is free of the doer and enjoyer. Therefore it is necessary to get rid of this wrong notion of doer and enjoyer.

One's Swarup or nature cannot be changed. E.g., The nature of fire is to give heat, light, and burn. We cannot change its nature to get cold fire. Since our nature or swarūpa is not bound by happiness or misery - Upanishads boldly declare that our nature is ever free or Nitya Mukta. Therefore we need to give up the attitude of doer and enjoyer.

Titiksha

"When understood deeply, painful experiences have a positive effect on our life." -Amma

Titiksha is the for bearance of the dualities ever-present in life. Unless one forebears such passing experiences of heat-cold, hunger-thirst, loss-gain, insult-praise and so on, all pairs of opposites will give trouble. In the absence of such forbearance, our practices to restrain the mind and senses, faith in the Guru and scriptures and our practices of concentration and meditation will not bear fruit.

In the Bhagavad Gita, Lord Krishna exhorts Arjuna to practice forbearance.

मात्रास्पर्शास्तु कौन्तेय शीतोष्णसुखदु:खदा: ।
आगमापायिनोऽनित्यास्तांस्तितिक्षस्व भारत ॥१४॥

यं हि न व्यथयन्त्येते पुरुषं पुरुषर्षभ ।
समदु:खसुखं धीरं सोऽमृतत्वाय कल्पते ॥१५॥

mātrā-sparśās tu kaunteya śītoṣṇa-sukha-duhkha-dāḥ
āgamāpāyino'nityās tans-titikṣasva bhārata
yam hi na vyathayantyete puruṣam puruṣarṣabha
sama-dukha-sukham dhīram so'mritatvāya kalpate
- Bhagavad Gita 2:14-15

Contact of the senses with the objects produces heat and cold, pain and pleasure. These experiences come and go, and are impermanent. Endure them! The firm person who is not affected by pain and pleasure, who remains equal-minded, surely is fit for immortality, O Arjuna!

Life is an endless stream of fleeting experiences. One who patiently forebears them, with even-mindedness and with the understanding that all such experiences are impermanent and do not affect his true Self-nature, such a person is free even here while alive in the body. Titiksha prepares one for this state of freedom.

Samadhāna

"When the mind becomes still through prolonged spiritual practices such as listening to satsangs, study of sacred books, selfless service and concentration, then it becomes possible to experience the ever-present hidden Truth." -Amma

Samadhāna is the prolonged one-pointedness of mind that is attained by the aspirant who practices Shama, Dama, Uparati and the rest. As mentioned earlier, the goal here is to develop the ability to stay even-minded and one-pointed which then enables the aspirant to deeply listen, without distraction to the pointing to the Self-nature by the instructions of the Guru and the Upanishads. Without such a one-pointed mind, those teachings fail to bear fruit.

Mumukshutwam

"Truth is always the most difficult thing, and at the same time, the easiest. For ignorant and egoistic people, it is the most difficult thing to know, and for those who are inquisitive and have a burning desire to know, it is the easiest." -Amma

Realization of Brahman the 'Sat' and negation of ignorance 'asat' is the true nature of oneself, the one who desires this intensely, is an aspirant (mumukshu). This is a higher stage from "Jigñasa," which means "the desire to know." Earlier, one had a "Jigñasa" regarding the world, but now, when the person understands that the world will not satisfy his or her needs for fulfillment and happiness, then there is a desire to know more about the alternative path. However, when one is convinced and intensely desires to be free, such a quest, such a state of mind is known as Mumukshatvam. In such a stage, with the accompanying Vairāgya or detachment, the aspirant is willing to put aside all distractions and obstacles to one's path and arranges one's life to enable sadhana.

We do practices and chant a mantra for some time, or we may meditate for some time, but we miss reality. We mistake these practices to end. Each has its importance, but there is a prescribed way of doing it for Self realization. When we do not follow it, we cannot realize the truth. Spiritual practices are like tools that can take us to the goal. But we have mistaken the tool to be the goal. Spiritual practices are meant for the purity of the mind. Firstly we should understand what the teaching is trying to say. In our minds, we should know about 'Sat.' Thus the discriminative mind realizes the Sat. When the mind has no subtleness or does not have the capacity, we should practice increasing its capacity. All spiritual practices are needed to increase eligibility. Non-duality inquiry needs inner purification, and all these practices should be done.

Conclusion

All the practices we discussed thus far is to create a tranquil, one-pointed mind that is able to grasp the pointer to the Truth. When this Truth is understood, there is no more doing. Once deep 'listening' occurs, the result is Knowledge. Self-realization occurs only through this knowledge of Sat, which is Beingness or Existence, the substratum of all. That is why the Vedantic scriptures repeatedly point out that realization is not the result of doing, not the result of spiritual practices. The spiritual practices are meant for inner purification, to get eligibility. In non-duality, the only effort needed is to learn about 'Sat.'

Names and forms are all unreal or imagined. Here imagined means it is experienced, but it is not real, or 'Sat.' Variety is seen in the ornaments, but the substratum is Gold. Here ornaments are unreal. 'Sat' is not sublated; that is why Sat is present in all states and all the time. What we experience in one state becomes sublated in another. What is present in one time is not present in another time. We should understand that this is not real. When we know this, then the unrealness of the world is understood.

What we have understood well in the discriminative mind, will then come to be our natural experience. First there is indirect knowledge and then direct knowledge takes place. When the Upanishads describe Brahman as Truth, Knowledge and Infinite is Brahman ('Satyam Jñānam Anantam Brahma'), it is indirect knowledge. Because it is attempting to describe the Truth about Sat but still not complete. On the other hand, 'Tat Twam Asi' is direct knowledge, because here Sat or Beingness is pointed to as one's real nature; like 'Sat you are,' the hearer will realize as 'Sat I am.' The purification of the mind through various practices is important. Then by hearing and reflecting, one gains knowledge. What is this knowledge? That the Self, the 'I' that one mistook to be associated with all sorts of labels is instead the infinite Self itself, which is undivided. The waking, dreaming and deep sleep states are mere appearances on Sat. Similarly, thoughts, perceptions, feelings, and experiences are happening in Self, the 'Sat' which is the substratum for all these.

When we say Self-realization, it is not like the experiences of the world. Reality is not anything like the concepts that we have. It is not that on some auspicious day, after a long duration of sadhana or spiritual practice, we will have the unique experience that 'I am Sat' or 'I am Brahman.' We have several such concepts. It is not an achievement. 'Sat I am' - is not a special status quo. The Self is not an experience. The 'I' is not perceived like we perceive sound, touch, form, taste, smell, etc. 'I' is Sat. Otherwise, the supreme reality, in whatever way we describe, becomes indirect. If we understand the supreme entity as separate, then we can never experience it as immediate and direct. It will always be far away. How can realization happen when we are praying to a supreme entity as separate? When we say the Self is immediate and direct, it does not mean visualization with our eyes. Self-awareness means knowing that 'I' am the nature of 'Sat.' We understand Sat as ever pure, all-pervasive. This understanding brings freedom. This is Self-realization.

ॐ

4

Vedanta sadhana - Atma vichara - Self-inquiry

"Because our minds are not pure, there is a constant flow of thoughts unrelated to God or our true self. Purity of mind is the precondition for the realization of the Truth. Only through sadhana can we avoid being enslaved by circumstances. We should learn the spiritual principles by listening to satsangs, and then live according to those principles. When the mind becomes still through prolonged spiritual practices such as listening to satsangs, study of sacred books, selfless service and concentration, then it becomes possible to experience the ever-present hidden Truth." -Amma

The purpose of the Upanishads

The Upanishads are the essence of the Vedas, the eternal scriptures of Sanatana Dharma. They are the revelation of the seers of Truth, this is why it is called the mother of all Knowledge. The entire purpose of listening to Upanishads is to know the reality, as they point directly to the Truth, which is the listener's Self. From childhood onwards, we have continually listened to so many things. Yet, nothing has liberated us, and we still feel we are bound. Everything we listened to, only served to condition us and added to our erroneous notions. We still feel miserable, so there is no use in continuing with our imaginations or someone else's imaginations.

Now we are seeking the help of the Upanishads to become free, through their very words of wisdom. Here, the Upanishads are not telling us something new about our true nature or twisting the truth, like describing a dog as a cat or a cat as a dog. Instead, it is pointing to the essential nature of things as they are, to the dog as a dog, and the cat as a cat.

Since our nature and nature of everything is the very 'Sat,' Existence and Awareness is the Truth. But we have forgotten this Truth due to ignorance or the influence of māya (cosmic illusion). This is making us believe that which is not true as the truth and Truth as not true. The Upanishads boldly negate all wrong concepts about ourselves and the world and make us arrive at this quintessence of Truth.

The Upanishads do not teach us about imaginary gods or saviors, like we are taught from our childhood in varying ways, depending on one's culture, religion and so on. People are usually taught to believe in a personal God, personal saviors and all sorts of fears are embedded in us to make us walk on the path of righteousness, to avoid hell and to support some imagined goal of going to heaven or to merge with a personal God.

This is not the perspective of the Upanishads. These customs adopted by the religions to guide the common masses are adopted according to the prevalent times, places and the people intended to be guided. If one happens to be born in such a society, then all the local tales, myths, beliefs and practices are then forced upon the person. All these practices are created and written with the intention of making us good human beings, but in the meanwhile, our freedom becomes disabled and crippled.

Through such circumstances, belief systems are born, leading to cults and religions, dividing humans into various classes and sects. Ultimately it may turn out good to some and bad to a majority as violence, intolerance, wars between different cults start. With this, all the so-called holy books, personal gods, all imaginations about freedom become a joke!

But when we start a sincere inquiry about questions such as 'why are we suffering? Why do humans hate each other? Who am 'I'? What is the relation between the Reality and 'me,' the separate self?' This is where discrimination about our true nature starts.

Because of ignorance, we make mistakes and create misery for ourselves and society. This has cost us dearly as we are not aware of our inner freedom. Now that which points to our inner Self and teaches us about our reality as Existence, Awareness and freedom from all misery is the way out. When we become aware of this fact with firm conviction about the Truth which is pointed, it brings freedom. All other religious beliefs and practices only aid to help bring us to this reality.

The Guru and the Upanishads do that job of pointing us to the Truth regarding our Self-nature and the world, so we should have shraddha (faith) in their words. This teaching regarding the Truth (Sat), negates the need for all personal Gods, saviors, beliefs and all conflicts and miseries. We should strive to know this Truth and to become free of ignorance regarding one's Self.

The prince who believed he was a hunter - a story

Once upon a time, a king was ruling the kingdom who had a new-born son. The powerful, neighboring king attacked his kingdom and could not resist this enemy. The minister of the kingdom realized that his king would be defeated, and he knew the enemy king would kill the king and his son. To save the future king and the kingdom, the minister took the child away from the country through a secret tunnel leading to the forest. There he handed over to the tribal chief of a group of hunters in the forest, to take care of the baby. There the boy grew up among the hunters. The boy learned the skills of hunting, jungle living and he was helping his hunter-father with various other tasks.

Meanwhile, the years passed, and now the boy was older and of the age where he could have been crowned the crown-prince of the kingdom. The minister returned to the forest where he had left the prince, and approached the prince and told him 'you are the prince of the nearby kingdom,' you are not the hunter-chief's son, you are not the one who has to hunt these animals for a living, instead you are the son of a king, your dynasty belongs to the lineage of sun dynasty and your ancestors were all kings, you should be the monarch for such dynasty.' The minister went on talking like this to the prince.

Hearing the minister's words, he learnt the truth and realized 'I am Prince who is supposed to be the king, I am not a hunter, I have to go back and rule the kingdom.' Thus he realized his true nature in that instance. Until then, he was not aware that he was a son of a king, that he was the Prince. But when told 'you are prince,' from that very moment he realized the truth and ignorance about his true self got cleared up.

Then they took him back to the kingdom and the Prince was made the king. Now he says' I am the king.' Here the knowledge, 'I am the king' is the most important factor for the cessation of all delusion. What actions did he have to undertake, to get that knowledge? Was there anything that had to be done to become the king? For him, no action was needed other than hearing, trusting and realizing the truth in the words of the minister.

It is possible the prince had doubts. Questions like 'how did I end up in the forest if I was son of a king? What about my parents in the forest?' etc. So he had to be told the whole story about the war, he was brought to the forest by escaping through the tunnel, his father the king getting killed in the battle, and all the details about his lineage had to be told. Other than telling him about his royal family lineage and the story of how he ended up in the forest, it was not necessary to perform any action to become king. When all the doubts were cleared, inside himself, he became aware 'I am a king, I only believed that I am a hunter because of ignorance.' It was the lack of awareness regarding his nature as Prince. Here the lack of awareness is a delusion. 'I am the son of a hunter' has been superimposed due to ignorance. That is not the reality. Like how light dispels darkness, the well-wisher's teaching about his essential nature dispelled his ignorance.

Was anything else needed to get rid of his ignorance? Like breath control, transcendental states of samādhi, or other practices like recitation, praying etc. No. Just listening to those words of the minister was enough. If he might have done anything further, it would only have been further enquire into those words of the minister like 'how did all this happen?' In that way, through question and answers, some more discussion and reflection would have taken place until his doubts, contrary thinking, and ignorance got negated. Then he got the conviction 'I am the Prince himself.' But only through the teaching did all his questions and ignorance get cleared.

To realize his identity as the Prince other than the negation of ignorance, nothing else was necessary. All his actions as a hunter end with the knowledge of his true identity. Simultaneously, all attachments are also dropped. To accomplish this, other than the teaching and teacher, nothing else was needed. No other practices were required. Similarly, this ignorance of 'Sat' or lack of knowledge regarding the Self is removed through the teachings about 'Sat.' In that fire of Knowledge, ignorance gets negated. Then all thoughts, sensations, perception, feelings like 'I am misery,' 'I am in bondage' 'I want peace' etc. which came because of identification with a name, body-mind-world complex get eliminated through right understanding. Ignorance of the indwelling Self is no more in oneself, and one remains as 'Sat,' as 'Brahman' alone. This conviction in 'Sat' is enough; nothing else is needed to realize this Truth. Knowledge replaces ignorance. Then one knows oneself as 'Sat.' Self-realization or Self-knowledge is all that is needed. For that, nothing else helps besides the teaching, the pointing to one's Self-nature. That is the role the Guru and the Upanishads play.

Shravana - listening

The Upanishads speak of our real nature as the Self. On hearing this, we should be able to drop our false conceptions and be in bliss. But, unfortunately, we feel we are the body, mind, senses, and intellect. Being oriented to the world outside, we feel separate or individual. From there, we go through endless cycles of pleasure and pain, which is finally just suffering. This vicious cycle is the ocean of transmigration.

If one discriminates between what is real and unreal, dispassion follows. Pursuit of the unreal leads to suffering. One who wants out of such suffering approaches a teacher with such questions. On seeing a sincere student, the teacher imparts the instructions that point to the seeker's essential nature. 'Sat' the ever, pure, Awareness and ever free of this limited thought as body-mind-world complex.

The Upanishads declare this Truth in various ways:

Tat twam asi- thou art That;

prajñānam Brahma - Awareness is Brahman;

Aham Brahmasmi- I am Brahman (Supreme Self);

Ayam Atmā Brahma - this Self (Atma) is Brahman;

Brahma Satyam Jagan Mithyā - Brahman is real; the world is illusory;

Brahma Satyam Jagat Satyam - Brahman is Real; the world also is real from the standpoint of the Self;

ekam evadvitīyam Brahma - Brahman is one, without a second;

Soham- He is I;

sarvam khalvidam Brahma - All of this is Brahman;

'na jāyathe' - 'Self is never born nor will it ever die;'

'nasato vidyate bhāvo nabhāvo vidyate satah' - 'The unreal never had Existence, and of the Eternal there is never cessation.'

Hearing these Truths turns the mind back to its source, and one's understanding regarding the Self transforms.

Such Self-knowledge negates ignorance. Cessation of ignorance means no more identifying with the unreal and limited. This body is born, goes through various stages, and finally dies while acquiring diseases. Being ever changing, it is unstable, hence unreal. In the same way, the mind experiences various thoughts, desires, emotions such as anger, pride, hatred, etc as well as feelings such as happiness, sadness, depression and fear. The nature of the mind is to constantly change, and it has no permanent state. Similarly, the intellect, vital force, senses, and world also are of the same character.

The Upanishads say one's true Self is the only Reality. As it never changes or ceases, it is never bound. Understanding this clearly, with a quiet, discerning mind enables us to understand these Truths. Knowing this clearly is a realization.

Manana - reflection

Our inability to perceive the Truth is because we are blinded by ignorance. Reflecting on the Upanishadic declarations of Truth helps us clear our doubts. Consistently doing this prevents the daily buildup of false concepts everyone acquires just by being in the world. Those who doubt the veracity of the teachings should first work to gain clarity about them. With such clarity, one gains experiences that eventually convince them that this is the Truth.

When we hear the Upanishadic words, we may have ignorance regarding the reality of our Self. So we might experience doubt regarding these teachings. This is because the world we experience through our senses, and the concepts we are conditioned with (samskāras) by long term interactions with the world, are in direct opposition to what the Upanishads expound. Through such thinking, we believe we are the body-mind-world complex, and that the Reality exists outside of us.

So questions often arise regarding the Upanishadic statements about the unreal nature of our experiences, and pointers to the Truth such as "Tat Twam Asi." These types of doubts arise when we realize the teachings do not correlate with our experiences in the world. Identifying ourselves to be a name, body, mind, senses, we cannot grasp Reality. Upanishads are pointing to our real Self as the Self of all, which is the Supreme Self.

So, reflection is necessary, where we deeply enquire into what we hear, through logic and using examples. This process is called manana or reflection.

When one is having the experience of a snake in a semi-darkness place, one is convinced that it is a snake. Only when someone comes and points out that it is a rope, do we lose our fear. So, the first instance of incorrect seeing gave us the experience of the snake. However, upon shining the light, one comes to know it is just a rope. So this 'light' of understanding is essential to dispel our ignorance.

Similarly, now we think of ourselves as 'I,' the individual as seer, listener, doer, thinker and the experiencer. This knowledge is made stronger by identifying with name, body, mind, senses, and world. In the same way, experiences follow in the form of happiness and misery, and all of this seems to be reality.

When one hears the truth about one's real nature from Upanishads, one's perspective changes, through further inquiry, one gets the conviction that he is of the nature of Sat, ever-present, ever pure, ever conscious, ever free Self.

By reflecting on the experience of dreams, we are able to understand our waking state as well clearly. The Self effulgent Awareness only appears as dream subjects, dream objects, and all dream world experiences. Along with dream space and time, the modulation of Awareness alone appears as a dream similarly waking state. Similarly, in the waking state, it is also the modulation of Consciousness appearing as the subject, objects, world, experiences, and time and space.

Then Awareness without modulating remains as such in the Deep sleep state.

Just like water modulates as waves, in the same way, waking and dream states are the modulations of 'Sat.' And just like water can exist without waves, similarly during deep sleep, 'Sat' remains naturally One, non-dual, without any modulation.

It is not just an individual feeling 'I'(aham buddhi) in the form of the knower (Pramatha) than oneself is. Instead, it is the very nature of the effulgence 'I' (swarūpam of aham buddhi). Therefore, the very existence, Awareness, and bliss are one's true nature.

It is not happiness that is to be gained. This Self nature of ours, is the very source of all happiness, because it does not come and go with the appearance, change, or cessation of mental modifications. It is ever free Awareness. It is not something to be practiced and gained; instead, it is the very nature of Self that is ever blissful.

Nididhyāsana - continuous meditation

"My children, the scriptures are the experiences of the rishis [Self-realized seers]. They cannot be grasped through the intellect. They can be realized only through experience." - Amma

In a prepared mind which is silent and one pointed, the words of the Guru and the Upanishads, when heard, creates in the listener the conviction that oneself is not the body-mind, etc and that his essential nature is ever free. However, sometimes this conviction does not develop and further enquiry is necessary in the form of reflection using logic along with deep, continuous meditation on the words of the Upanishads. Sometimes, there is conviction that develops, but it is weak and due to the bad habits developed over multiple lifetimes where one has functioned with the erroneous self-belief of being the body-mind. This results either in doubt, or a discontinuous on and off pattern where the aspirant tends to revert to past habits of erroneous identification. In order to create the stable conviction so that one functions from the correct understanding of being the Self, and is unshaken amidst the interactions with the body-mind-world complex, continuous meditation (nididhyāsana) is of tremendous help.

Ignorance is nothing but the belief that one is a separate individual represented by the body-mind, the 'I am so-and-so' belief. When the upanishadic instructions create a frame of reference for this 'I', which is the Self, one might still succumb to reverting to the erroneous belief due to habits. In that case, we have to contemplate with one-pointedness in oneself without any external aids. With a meditative mindset, we have to reflect within ourselves as 'I' the Atma is ever free, unattached. In me (Atma), ignorance, sorrow, delusion, fear do not exist.

I am That Self (Atma), who is free of all the modifications of body, mind and Prana.

In Self, there is no hunger and thirst.

I am neither born nor going through various stages to finally die. I am the immortal Self. Nothing can kill me, nor am I going to kill, as there is no second to Atma. I am pure Self.

I am free of diseases that affect the body.

I am free of all mental modifications, such as virtues or vice. I am free of sin, untainted Self I am.

I am free of all classes, caste, creed, and various stages of lifestyle.

I am unattached, ever effulgent, which ignorance cannot eclipse. I am infinite, immortal, and blissful.

Through such deep reflection, along with resting in one's Awareness of 'I am' free of all labels, one creates the correct, new habit of functioning as the Self. Like Amma says - 'Know your Self by discrimination between Sat and Asat', that is, always identify with your essential Self nature, and never forget what is not-Self, which is the body-mind-world complex. Each mood, feeling, sensation, and perception that arise in our mind due to our latent tendency to time is checked by discrimination.

When we perceive anything, either a mental modification or an object in the world, we say 'my knowledge' 'I' know, these are mind, intellect modification. This modification includes thoughts, sensations, feelings about oneself as body, mind, intellect, senses, and this world from gross to subtle. In both the waking and dream states, various such modifications take place. If one functions as the ego, all of these modifications are grasped at with likes and dislikes, that is, through the lens of one's preferences. If we enquire, 'To whom is this knowledge known? Who experiences these modifications?,' we may say 'to me.' Here the 'I' became a subject which is the individual-self, the perceiver of all modifications. But who is that, who experiences all these cognitions, including individual self (the ego)? When this is inquired, we realize that it is the Atma, the Self. This subject grasps, knows, the mind. In Self, all these appear.

The mind is consciousness - like light mixed with shadow. In sunlight, if a Pole is placed, a shadow is formed. Wherever obstacles come, the shadow is formed due to limiting adjuncts. In that case, the sun cannot express itself fully, so the shadow is formed. Shadow means not complete darkness nor full light. Still, it is under the presence of light that such shadows are formed. The mind is the limiting adjunct; in other words, it is modulation in 'Sat.'

Like how the shadow is formed in light due to obstruction, similarly the mind is like a shadow caused due to ignorance of Self. It is subtle in nature. The light coming through the mind is nothing but effulgence of the Self (Atma Prakashan). Due to erroneous identification, the mind becomes a mix of light and darkness.

When knowing takes place, it is both Self-experience and objective experience. To see the shadow, we take the help of light. In this example, the light is self-effulgent, but for the shadow, light is necessary. Similarly, the mind has a light, but it is a dim light, like a shadow. In every cognition, 'Sat' is revealed but not entirely because of the mix between Self (Atma) and non-self (anātman). The knot of Consciousness and inert (Chit-Jada granthi) exists as if it cannot be separated. Only the knower of Reality (Tattwa Jñani) can separate it, but not possible for others. Like the mythical swan, which drinks only milk leaving water, the knower of Self always separates the Self from non-self with discrimination.

For the ignorant, even though it is available to be known, still it is not known because of identification with the non-self. The mind becomes an obstacle to Self-effulgence. Like how shadows appear when the sunlight gets obstructed due to clouds, or even as night comes when the earth turns away from light, creating darkness. When clouds get clear, the shadow disappears, and then light without obstacles shines clearly, fully.

This is how our experience is. If a cloud comes in between the sun, then we cannot see. The situation of the mind is like this. When the mind clears, 'Sat' is revealed as it is Self-effulgent. The Supreme Self alone is shining. When we try to experience Self therein, however, the mind comes and obstructs.

When the obstruction of the mind is negated, there ends the seer, the seen and the act of sight, and only 'Sat' without obstacle shines. The light of Awareness is the seer of everything, in this light, the shadow-like mind light is seen. All modifications are names and forms continuously seen. Awareness knows them all. Continuously all modifications are known in one form in one light. The mind is known continually. Still, it cannot be full light as long as we see the shadow. It cannot become full light because of the limiting adjunct. Just like the shadow pole is the reason for the shadow, likewise the mind is the reason, i.e., the inert part of the mind is the reason for the ignorance of 'Sat.' 'Sat,' although ever-present, is not found. Even though it is ever-present, still and known, it is not known to us. It is like a shadow where we don't see only light. In the same way, since the mind always wanders, we are not aware of 'Sat.'

The Self is available in every cognition. It is like only light without shadow. It is available every second, ever immediate and direct. That is why here also it is said to be the seer of all cognitions. Beyond both available and not available through which only this 'Sat' is known. In the waking state, all objectified knowledge is known. Whenever the objectified knowledge appears, that knowledge is cognized. To whom this cognition happens, when this is inquired, we say, 'it is to me.' I am the cognisor of all the cognitions and witness for all cognitions, which is ever effulgent. That is why it is described to be ever available and direct. Revelation is its very nature, and it cannot change its 'Sat' nature, which is immediate and direct.

Sat is ever shining, ever available, ever knowing. Its intrinsic nature is to be the cognisor of all cognitions. Sat is Self-effulgent in nature and very much aware of itself. All thoughts, sensations, perceptions, and feelings exist in the Self, shining in its presence and acting like a cover or obstacle due to which it cannot discern. So, this is what we should clear up, and for this, only discrimination is needed.

Through each cognition, it is this Self-effulgence which is revealed, discerned and being realized. 'Sat' by nature is direct and immediate.

So through Shravana, Manana and Nididhyāsana (Listening, reflection and contemplation) about the real, one gets conviction of Reality. Darkness goes by light, so it is negligible. Therefore, there is no need to describe darkness; all efforts to describe darkness are waste. Because it is not an object, that is why it is called indescribable. Usually, in the world, to destroy a thing, a lot of effort is necessary. For darkness, no effort is necessary, it disappears in the light. In the presence of sunlight, darkness disappears. In the same way in the presence of Self-effulgence Sat, this mind fades away. As it is negligible, it is said not by effort, nor by people's strength nor by any action, it is possible. Instead, it is possible only by negating various false concepts regarding 'Sat.' Therefore, 'Sat' experience is available in every cognition, such as thoughts, sensations, perceptions, modifications, and metal modes. If it is so clear, then what is the obstacle for realization? Our concepts regarding realization are the obstacle. We have many resolutions and concepts about a realization; otherwise, there are no obstacles. 'I will realize now' is the concept that is the obstacle for realization. The Self is not an object, yet we make our concepts, 'this is how I will realize.' I will experience this,' 'experience will be like this,' and so on. However, in Reality, words, speech cannot reach what 'Sat' is all about. To put effort into the mind and use words to know this is not possible. The Self is a seer of all modifications. It is revealed continuously in all cognitions. This being so, we cannot think of 'I will understand it' as the goal. It is the substratum for all.

The realization that we cannot catch 'Sat' by concepts is the end of all efforts. By discrimination, calmness in the mind comes. However, the calmness is not the end in itself, because even in deep sleep, the mind is calm. Even in samādhi, the transcendental state, we achieve calmness to a certain limit. Yet, the obstacle of the mind is not cleared when we return to the waking state. It is only by discrimination of the Self from the non-self, does the mind no longer distract from the Self. By the Self, it shines and this Self is never lost sight of.

In every cognition, the 'Sat' alone is the most obvious. It is the one experienced in each cognition. That is why in all cognitions, the Self alone is revealed (known). It is the true experience, as it is the inner Self of all modification. All waking states, dream states experience change. All experiences appear and cease in 'Sat,' the Self, and witness of all these.

Due to the influence of the illusionary mind, the Self loses focus on itself and instead identifies with the modulations of the body-mind-world complex. When the wind stops blowing, waves become calm, only still water remains, then we cannot differentiate water from waves. Similarly, when the mind becomes calm, only 'Sat' remains and there is no more the seer of all modulations. This is where the calmness of mind helps in recognizing Sat. Yet, it does not mean we are suppressing the mind or controlling according to our concepts. The mind calms down by itself through the practice of discrimination, the recognition that the movements, the cognitions are not-Self. The mind thus becomes calm by the right knowledge, through discrimination. Knowledge is not an action to stop it because discrimination is not an action. Awareness is not action; instead, it is free of action.

In yoga practice, one strives to still the modifications of the mind. However, the quietude of mind achieved through the practice of separating Self from non-Self is different from the stillness achieved through the practice of yoga, because one abides in the Self, that is the essence behind the mind's functioning. The mind's indwelling Self-nature is free of action. It was understanding the mind's nature, which is 'Sat' in all cognitions. Witness to all cognitions, that knower is the 'Sat' himself. One has to understand the witness to all modulations. There is no mind apart from 'Sat,' i.e., it is beyond action, qualities, the class. That is why all experiences are in the realm of ignorance of Self, and its attributes will not touch the witness. Like light is not affected in the room when all activities take place.

Similarly, in Self or Sat, which is seer of all modulations, whether mind moves or not, there is no importance anymore. Sat cannot be sublated. The body-mind-world complex nature cannot affect 'Sat,' the Self. That is why it is said, they are superimposed, imagined, like how mirage-water does not affect land. No imagined entity can affect Reality. Whether we see movement in water or no movement in the water, it is always just water. There is nothing apart from water. If at all there is anything other than water, then we say there was wind. Likewise, in the mind, whether the modulations are seen or not, it is still 'Sat' alone. There is no otherness in 'Sat.' All modulations in the body-mind-world complex are 'Sat' only. There is no second in 'Sat.' If we have to say something is there, then it is ignorance.

With this right perspective, we should see everything; in the right knowledge. The inner nature of the mind is calmness. Like how the fire is light, fire is heat by nature, and there are no distinctions like fire and light. Here the inner Self of all cognitions is Self alone. In the Self, these exist. In all modifications and every cognition, only 'Sat' is revealed (known). All modifications are getting revealed, realized - that is 'Sat' himself, oneself is the 'Sat' the Atma. One understands as 'I' the 'Sat' in body, mind, and intellect is how one links with everything and knows himself by discrimination. One knows Reality, which is free of body, mind, intellect... is the right knowledge. If one understands once, there will be change; otherwise, it is an illusion or imagination about realization. Here we are talking about non-dependent right understanding. Self-satisfaction and negation of sorrow come not by concepts but through the right knowledge. The nature of 'Sat' is ever-present and free. There is no bondage, free from body, mind, intellect, and this is liberation. 'Mine', 'I' is not there separately in 'Sat.' He alone is in all body, no personal liberation. Self is absolute Consciousness. The rest is all imagined by the ignorant.

There is no personal liberation. It is not confined to someplace and time. Space is undivided despite pot, cave, and the building is getting accommodated. Similarly, Consciousness is one in nature; from waking to sleep, it is one undivided Consciousness. There is no individual Self, no wise, no ignorant. It is 'one Sat' as if it is witness and substratum to all cognitions which are modulating like 'I know 'I do not know.' Till now, all concepts act as obstacles in the form of ignorance, attachment, bondage, liberation are being told by revealing the truth.

When natural errors are cleared, then the witness of all cognition is revealed as a hearer of hearing, thinker of thought, the scene's sear, knower of all knowledge, and knower of all experiences.

In Reality, it is different from known, unknown, and beyond. It is not recognized by way of its appearance because it is 'Sat.'

By discrimination, it is known in each cognition. All are modulations in 'Sat'and 'chit.' That is why, as an object, it is not to be known. In every thought, it is known; in every knowledge, it is known; one cannot be different from knowing.

In the 'Sat,' it is the eye of the eye, the ear of the ear, it is seer of all cognitions. It is not like seeing a book where 'I' is separate. The book is separate. It will be mistaken if we say 'seen' is different, 'sear' is different. To prevent this mistake as a 'seer' of objects, it is the 'Sat' in all cognitions like thoughts, sensations, and perceptions.

When we see a book, we should know the inner Self of the book in 'Self.' In 'Sat' book appears, in one's Reality, in one's substratum, everything is superimposed. If we cannot know the book as the Self (the Reality) appearance, that means we do not know the Reality of the book. Still, we know the only book. That is why when we see things, we are seeing them through their Reality. When we see fire, we know fire's nature burns to give light and spread splendor. Here when we know through the object, that means we know through the very Self of that object. 'Sat,' as the nature of wave is water, nature of ornament is gold, nature of pot is mud. Likewise, the nature of all objects is 'Sat,' chit.' Like Light, heat, splendor is fire, sat, chit, Ananda is the Self, known as Self of all, is not just witness like 'sear' is different 'seen.' Still, it is the inner Self where we cannot separate 'sear' from 'seen.' Because when we see the book, we divide the 'knower' of the book from the book known.' We say my book, your book, destroyed book, etc. this was when we were to see the book as different. Here we are not talking of effort to see the book as separate or see something different.

We are saying we cannot separate 'witness' from the 'witnessed' that is 'knower' from the 'know,' which is the book as cognition is also Consciousness. Here it is not telling to discover or put effort into finding 'knower' from these cognitions. It is not telling us to realize cognition like 'knower of the consciousness' from the above said 'cognition,' it is not asking us to find out. We are experiencing the continuity of the knower the 'Sat' in all cognitions.

That sometimes comes like an illusion, doubt, ignorance, and say 'I am knowing,' 'I am not knowing,' 'I forgot.' All these are different modulations of 'Sat.' All these together are called cognitions. 'This knowledge is clear to me,' 'this knowledge is not clear to me,' or we say 'this knowledge is confirmed,' 'with form,' 'without form' all these expressions are part of modulations of 'Sat.' These are different forms of knowledge. It is not in one form. Knower illumines different objects, like the book, table, chair, all the world. According to objects, their knowledge, the knower nature also changes, as doubts, like forgetfulness, remembering, etc. The changing forms of this knowledge are modulations in the knower then something that is not changing one is the 'Sat' the knower. If we separate the knower from modulations in knowledge like rising and fall. Then without change, one is there that is the knower. The objective forms when discarded, negated then what remains is Consciousness. Like waves when negated water remains.

That Consciousness is one with a witness. Water is one. Therefore, we said the inner Self of cognition is the 'Sat.'

Like the inner Self of a wave is water; otherwise, we are deluded in this rise and fall of cognitions and try to realize something new. The Reality of this Consciousness, when it is identified with various objects, is called objective knowledge. Like a chair, a table like waves in water. Still, the Self in every cognition is 'Sat.'

There is no knower of consciousness. It is Self-aware. Again, when it is said, each thought and sensation is not separate from the Self, one is not to make effort to perceive the Self in them. What is pointed out is that these thoughts and sensations are like the modulation of water, and we are to be attentive of the seer of all cognitions. The mud does not seek to understand every pot made with it, it knows all pots are not different from it. This effortless Self-awareness is what is pointed out here.

This only he says 'I' the Self, always knowing himself as that which is not dependent on anything (nirapēksha), like 'seer of scene,' 'hearer of hearing,' 'conscious of consciousness,' there is no individual. There is no need because the very nature of Consciousness is the realization. Knowledge is needed to remove misunderstanding, illusions about Consciousness and eliminate this ignorance and doubts.

Realization is peanuts

'Realization is just like peanuts for me'.- Amma

What does Amma mean by the word 'peanuts' here?

All our cognition can be deduced to thoughts, sensations, feelings, and perceptions. In all these cognitions, it is the Self, the Existence (Sat) alone that is revealed, just like in all orna-ments - gold alone exists, and in all pots - clay alone exists, in all waves - water alone exists. Like how the screen is the substratum for all pictures to appear, similarly, Sat alone is the witness and substratum for all cognitions.

For the sun, from its own perspective, there is no darkness as there are no obstructions in its illumination. That is why there is no day, afternoon, evening, or night to the sun. But from the observer's perspective, there is day, afternoon, and night. And even a trivial obstruction, such as clouds, a thumb, eyelids, or a cataract in an eye can create darkness. But, of course, all these obstacles are only from the individual's standpoint. From the sun's stand point, all these are negligible as the sun's self effulgence is free of darkness.

Likewise, Sat is ever free of the superimposition of name, body, mind, senses, intellect, and world. But for one who is ignorant about this reality, all these act as obstacles and cause the experience of misery and bondage. In reality, Sat is ever free in all three states and three periods of time. This is the right knowledge. All 'asat' nature gets negated in this right knowledge. If one has this conviction all the time, that itself is Self-realization or Ishwara sakshathkāram. From this understanding, the perceived reality of all experiences are only from ignorance. All these are continuously changing as they have no reality in themselves. Thus, limited experiences are negligible in understanding Sat's infinite, conscious, immortal nature.

This inevitable truth (Sat) is what our beloved Amma means by the word 'peanuts.' This is also what Sri Shankaracharya's statement of "It is as clear as a gooseberry in the palm" stands for. One can never miss it if one possesses this right discrimination.

Why do most people in the waking state experience themselves as 'I am happy, 'I am miserable,' 'I am ignorant,' 'I am knowing,' 'I am not knowing,' etc., when they are in reality, the 'Sat,' the Self, and free of all these attributes? It is because of a lack of inquiry. So, the reality - the Sat is not experienced even though it always exists as ever free. The ignorance about this reality makes them feel like a samsāri, an individual bound with a multitude of sufferings with specks of happiness.

One of the direct ways out of this is to enquire into our three states. Since, during the waking state, we are entangled with the I, mine, and the world. So, we are asked to look into deep sleep initially. In a deep sleep, even though most people feel that 'I didn't know anything about it or there is nothing, no one is able to deny that they existed and were peaceful during that time. Hence this Sat, pure existence as one's natural state is pointed out. In a deep sleep, Sat alone exists and is one with the Self. Because of this oneness, there is no experience of even Sat or any other worldly experience. Here one is naturally happy and peaceful as there is no second to know. Here one abides in Self naturally without any discrimination.

Then in the dream, the same Sat itself manifests as both the dreamer and the dream.

This does not solve the problem of ignorance one faces in the waking state. The question then arises, If our ever-free nature exists only in deep sleep and the Self is bound during the waking state, then why is the Self declared Self to be ever free?

The Truth is, the Self in waking state is also ever free. Yet, one feels bound due to a lack of the above knowledge and discrimination. He superimposes the limitations of body, mind, intellect, and world around with various experiences on the pure Sat. This limited feeling is like a shadow where partial light and partial darkness appear mixed together. The mind with innumerable cognitions comes in between and causes an eclipse, bringing in various experiences like happiness and misery. In this way, one gets identified with these experiences and relates to the body, mind, and world complex. This is how an individual self appears and experiences samsāra endlessly. Such a person strives for freedom, happiness, peace, but instead, he gets tossed up and down and says 'I am the doer' 'I am the enjoyer' 'I am ignorant' 'I am knowledgeable' etc.

When one identifies with the body, he says, 'I am fat' 'I am thin' 'I am healthy' 'I am diseased' etc. On identification with the mind, he says whatever happens to the mind, it is happening to himself like 'I am sad,' 'I am miserable,' 'I am happy,' 'I am lost', 'I am angry,' 'I am humble' etc. On identification with the intellect, he says, 'I have decided,' 'I have not decided.' Identifying with the senses, he says, 'I am blind,' 'I am deaf,' 'I am not tasting,' 'I am not smelling' etc. Similarly, when one identifies with the world's nature, he feels it is happening for or to himself. Thus one goes through continuous changing experiences like aversions, feelings of hatred, likes, dislikes, etc. All of these are nothing, but superimpositions on the ever-free Sat only.

Despite the Truth, the Sat being pointed out, the problems don't seem to end. It is because of identifying Sat with asat nature. This misidentification leads one to say 'body is real,' 'world is real,' and 'mind is conscious.' In saying that the 'mind is conscious,' misidentification starts. One says they are the knower and experiencer of all thoughts, sensations, and perceptions. This misidentification of superimposition is like an eclipse, leading him to alternate feelings that one is conscious and ignorant about the truth. One is unable to come out of this vicious cycle of confusion.

The real aspirant is one who recognizes his own drawback, condition of helplessness, and ignorance combined with a zeal to become free in one's life. This aspirant approaches the master, the guru who has realized the Truth, the Self with an attitude of humility and surrender. Such an aspirant becomes a seeker of Truth and a right disciple who desires to realize the Self through right knowledge. The master, seeing this intense desire in the aspirant, starts instructing him about the wisdom of truth. This paves the way for discrimination between Sat and asat. This starts the rectification of one's time immemorial superimposition error. Where one was superimposing limited self-sufferings over the unlimited Sat, now with discernment, one gets rid of his doubts, contrary thinking, and ignorance regarding Self.

This discrimination between real and unreal makes him understand reality. In the light of this right knowledge, he will come to know that Self alone is known in each and every cognition. This releases the aspirant from the misery caused due to ignorance, which is technically called liberation from samsāra.

That is why Amma uses the word 'peanuts' to show that Sat is our natural state, and all the while we are Sat, and it is this simple Truth we need to understand in a simple way.

Self as the substratum

"The Paramatman (Supreme Self) is everywhere. It is not a distant entity. The Paramatman is truly 'nearer than the nearest.' Children, you may search for God everywhere, but He is closer to you than you could ever imagine. Shake off your identification with the body and, transcending it, wake up in Awareness; then you will realize that God is 'nearer than the nearest.'" -Amma

Take anything, like the objects around, whatever you see or hear. As oneself, which is usually taken to be the body, mind, senses, intellect and to start exploring— what is the material which made 'me' as subject and 'not me' as an object? What exactly is it?

Is it separately two different things or one whole picture consisting of 'world as outside of me' and 'me as body, mind, senses intellect?'

Or is it that they appear in one Awareness, where Awareness as the screen enlivens all pictures as 'me' and 'not me?'

So, for all these to appear, there should be something to embrace. What is it - no matter whether you give it a name or not, which is the pure existence for all the pictures to appear? It is the light of pure Awareness that enables all-knowing, for the knowledge to take place regarding all pictures as 'me' and 'not me.' That means it is the very source - the Self, which is ever free from all these appearances as 'me' and 'not me.' They come and go from time to time, which is revealed when colored with that effulgence of Reality!

With this exploration, we see clearly, or we are becoming aware that the one Reality modulating as 'me' and 'not me' is the one whole infinite Reality!

Reality of the world

"Happiness comes from within. A dog will bite a bone and think that the energy it gets from the blood of its own wounded gums is from the bone. We are also similarly deluded when we think that the bliss we get from within is coming from an external object." -Amma

Reflect on your dreams,
There is no cause and effect.
No psychic power—all illusion!
Even this waking state now is a similar dream!
Turiya, which is one's Self, is the seer of dream and waking state,
All of this, all that is perceived is a modulation of Awareness, Turiya spandana.
Waking, Dream, Deep sleep,
That Turiya you are,
You are that Turiya,

114

The one who is listening to these Śruti words is the one who is Turiya!

Like tat twam asi, You are that ever free Self!

The one who is listening, 'you are the 10th man' is the one whom this is addressed to, not someone else!

Upanishad says it in a simple, direct manner.

We also should understand directly and in a simple way as That twam asi points to our real ever free nature.

By hearing Upanishad know illusion as an illusion. This is what the rope mistaken to be a snake example refers to.

Instead, we impose reality to unreal experiences,

What is real is your Paramārthika swarūpam, the Inner Self

That Arivu, that understanding is what is pointed out here as you, the Paramārthika swarūpam.

You, as Atma, are accurate.

Not as name and forms,

All names and forms should be negated; they will get negated in reality.

If you take all these current experiences in the waking state as accurate, then what is the cause of this waking state?

You say 'the previous waking.'

If I then ask 'how the previous came?,' you would say ' from the last,' then the loop is endless.

This is a logical fallacy! (Infinite regression)

Then if I ask -Which is the first waking state? First fate? First jīva? No answer. So there is no such first!

It is all nice to hear the word first, but no such thing. So it is called māya Anirvachanīyam! Indescribable!

So, where is the beginning of our world or creation?

The Chandogya Upanishad says, 'it is Existence which is in all three periods.'

Not as a name or form.

As Existence, the Awareness, we are eternal!

That is our true nature,

Not as this body, mind, intellect, world.
So it is an illusion like a snake,
There is no answer to where it came from,
But we are happy with the illusion.
From one illusion to another illusion, we move!
From one waking experience to another waking experience!
From one dream to another dream!
So in whatever way it appears in that manner, it is not real.
Our existence we superimpose on this and feel real.

The effulgence of existence and Awareness is seen in all experiences, but we mistake them as mere experiences.

It is light in your room expressing in each experience of the object, but we are not aware of light, only of the objects we see.

Switch off the light!

Do you see the object?

If it was present in whatever way it appears when there is light, then now also in darkness too, we should have its experience,

Why, then, do we not experience objects in the same way?

Because of the light's existence, it is the light's effulgence which is seen through objects,

Not the objects as such.

Similarly, now our body, mind, senses, intellect, the world is nothing but the effulgence of Existence and Awareness!

In deep sleep, we are one with Existence.
Now we see that Existence in all variety,
Never does Existence cease.
But names and forms cease in deep sleep.
So the Truth is Existence.
We are That.
You are That. Tat twam asi!

My meditation

"The goal of meditation is to make the agitated mind peaceful and still. When thoughts cease through meditation, the mind becomes more pure and subtle. The mind becomes more tuned to the rhythm of the universe. In that stillness, the unknowable knowledge becomes knowable." -Amma

My real nature is 'ever free' and 'ever pure.' That is a firm conviction. This is my meditation.

Understanding this Truth is by the grace of thy lotus feet, on which is my meditation.

The gap where 'I' was feeling unaccomplished is filled with ever-established Self-nature (nitya shuddha Atma Swarūpam) without any doubt. Such is my meditation.

From that satisfaction arise fulfillment and peace under the power of thy grace. This is all that is my meditation.

As a way of paying respect to the knowledge, I try to convey the same knowledge to others, as it brought about a conviction. It is my meditation and reflection to purify my mind.

When I look back, I acknowledge and realize the fact that you have given me a place and shelter at thy lotus feet. It fills me with gratitude. All this is my Meditation.

I am an ordinary person with all body limitations and a mind trying my best to serve you in whatever possible way. Thy grace alone is helping and guiding me in dealing with all the external worldly situations. Remembering this with gratitude, is my meditation.

I strive to be careful that whatever Loka Vyavahāra (inter-action with the world) happens from my side should happen without disturbing others. And that is my meditation.

Despite all my effort, some things may not work out due to my negligence, and consequently, certain people may be hurt.

So I take refuge at thy lotus feet to correct myself by asking forgiveness. This is my meditation.

You are my Guru in imparting the eternal Truth to me. Therefore, I meditate on thy lotus feet, which are the very substratum for all that Is.

'O Guru, the 'sat' in me and you and everything is one whole 'sat,' where all differences persist without 'sat' ever getting tainted. This is my meditation.

Differences are there at a relative level. So 'You as guru' and 'me your disciple,' 'world around with variations.' But in Reality, it is the one Truth which is 'sat. So all the differences cease at thy lotus feet. Thus 'I' meditate on thy lotus feet, surrendering my body, mind, and speech.

Māya is just negligible in this 'sat.' It cannot ever overpower 'sat,' the Reality of everything. This is my meditation.

You are the Avatar who came as promised in your previous incarnations. This is my Meditation.

My meditation is to see all human beings, nature, animals, and the entire creation as 'sat.'

Let this meditation be not just for a few moments, Mother. Please bless me that my meditation should last until this body falls. May all my activities become meditation at thy lotus feet.

Conviction in 'sat'

"Either proceed according to God's will, convinced that "Everything is You," or inquire "Who am I?" with the strong conviction that "Everything is within me." -Amma

It is 'sat' appearing "as though" It has taken the form of the Guru. Then, it is 'sat' again "as though" It has taken the form of the disciple.

This 'sat' alone is modulating Itself as the Guru and disciple and all the variations in the world. Because of the limiting adjuncts such as mind, body, intellect, the form seems different as a guru, disciple, and the world. But in truth, it is one 'sat' only.

'Sat' when modulating in various names and forms will function following the behavior of that form. It is like clay appearing as a pot, plate, or cup, which functions according to its form. But in reality, they are all clay, stripped of all names, forms, and actions they perform.

It's like the electricity which runs a fan, a light, a grinder, etc., which have different functions serving different purposes. Still, the Reality is electricity itself is free of any action.

'Sat' appears as the mother, and the same 'Sat' appears as the child. Mother has to discipline the child, and the child has to listen to the mother and behave according to the mother's advice. None is superior or inferior; both the mother and the child grow together performing their duty, helping each other's needs. But the Reality is 'sat' in mother instructs and 'sat' in child listens, thus it seems 'sat' alone is playing all the game. But 'sat' itself is free of all games. 'sat' is also free of all superimposed relationships.

Discriminating people know the Truth, but the ignorant ones are not aware of it.

'Sat' in Guru and 'Sat' in a disciple is one whole Sat. Still, the Guru instructs, guides, loves, cares, and takes responsibility to make disciples aware of that 'Sat.'

'Sat' has been in existence before creation. It exists now, and it is 'Sat' alone, the truth in all names and forms. 'Sat' as Guru proclaims the truth, and 'Sat' as disciple surrenders to the Guru's lotus feet. 'Sat' in the disciple takes the guidance to become aware of its true nature to be 'sat' alone.

As the teaching, as the Guru, as a hearer, as an aspirant, as the scripture, It is 'sat' alone that is modulating.

As the Divinity, as the devotee, as the master, as the servant, as the friend, 'sat' alone is modulating,

As me, as you, as the universe, like the manifest, as the unmanifest sat is modulating,

As conviction in discriminative minds, as ignorance in the ignorant, 'sat' alone is modulating.

As a blessing in me, as grace, as pearls of wisdom 'sat' alone, is modulating in infinite ways.

ॐ

5

Satguru

"A Satguru possesses a visible physical form as well as an invisible spiritual presence. The visible form is important. However, the invisible presence is the most important. When the wind blows, the branches and leaves of a tree move. That reveals the wind's form. However, the presence of the wind is everywhere and is all-pervasive. This is the difference between the Satguru's physical form and their spiritual presence." -Amma

What is the role of the Guru in our lives? Is such a Guru necessary? What does the Guru expect from us? Can we depend on a Guru for guidance in life? Such questions frequently arise.

Guru means one who removes the darkness of ignorance regarding oneself.

We all have had many Gurus until now, as we are always learning. We learn something everyday.

All the knowledge we possess is accumulated through personal experiences, books, teachers, family and friends. Thus, in regard to our personal life or worldly life, all these mediums are constantly helping us. Even our mind acts as a medium to improve our knowledge to do better in our life.

So whatever guides us in life becomes our Guru. To learn, we should be open without any prejudice. Then one even starts to learn from nature and inanimate objects.

On the spiritual path, the Guru plays a vital role. The Upanishads are the words of the Guru. Guru is not a personality.

Yet, we pray to get blessings and to make our minds stronger to listen to His wisdom. But the Guru is the light of wisdom. His words will remove ignorance from our hearts.

What is this ignorance? We believe our lives are limited. Or we believe that the meaning or purpose of life is to go to heaven, or to accumulate pleasures, experiences, wealth, possessions and power, and we define the achievement of these as 'success.' Thus our lives are caught between the dualities of happiness and suffering.

But this is not the Truth. Our true nature is free of misery. Due to our erroneous assumptions, we misperceive reality, like seeing mirages in the desert, or to mistake a rope for a snake in the dark. Thus, our whole life, we suffer in one sense or another by assuming ourselves to be limited.

Yet the Upanishads point to our Self as ever-free pure Awareness. That we are full by nature without Death! And the nature of our real Self is Immortal!

So all our assumptions regarding Life and Death, pain and pleasure are negated.

This line of Guru's lineage from time immemorial talks about this Truth and liberates us from ignorance regarding our true nature. And this will continue till as long as this creation lasts!! The Guru parampara, or the lineage of Gurus, will last forever.

Whoever listens to the Guru's words will become free of the disease of saṃsāra (life and death or ocean of transmigration)

He realizes he is ever free, and becomes free from the erroneous belief that he is the one who was born one day and will die one fine day.

Thus, the importance of the Guru has always been emphasized in our spiritual life.

Guru pādam

"A Mahatma, or Satguru, has transcended all vasanas, (inborn negative tendencies) by controlling all desires and thought waves. This is what gives them the power to smile heartily and simply enjoy being the witness to everything. As they are a source of eternal bliss and happiness, faith in the Satguru helps to make you truly happy and content – to make your life a festive celebration." -Amma

When we embark on a long journey, we frequently stop to check how far we have come and how much longer it will take us to reach our destination. We look for signposts that guide us in the right direction and adjust our travel speed to complete our journey on time. In addition, we stop to refuel our fuel tanks and can also have the luxury of a meal stop enroute depending on the distance that needs to be covered in our journey.

We have been on a long odyssey for many lifetimes to know ourselves in much a similar way. In this long journey, right from our waking moments until we fall asleep, we are engaged in trying to know ourselves in everything from repeated births to deaths. The nature of this journey is that we do not know how much more ground we need to cover to reach our destination. Therefore, we drag our feet taking long breaks in the world of ignorance. If we ask when this search began and when it will end? The Upanishads say that it is beginningless (anādi). Still, it will end (antham) when we reach the Guru Pādam, the holy lotus feet of our Sadguru.

For this rewarding journey, we need the grace of the Guru, scriptures, Ishwara, and our minds. The Guru is ever compassionate and wants only our progress in our spiritual journey. His blessings are always with us. His words are scriptures, by which he provides insight to the disciple regarding his Self nature and to progress in sadhana. In our case, Ishwara himself, in the form of the Guru, has come to us and is providing conducive circumstances to complete our journey. Finally, our mind plays a vital role in taking all these blessings and sustaining on this path without getting disturbed or distracted. With everybody's blessings, we will analyze what we are doing to get more clarity. Indeed, it is refueling the mind, being more energetic, more receptive to the Master.

Usually, we are focused on the world, always seeking to expand our sense of "I" and "mine" through possessions, relationships, wealth, name, and fame. Our ego is identified with this pursuit for many births. When we come to receive Amma's darshan after leaving these ingrained trappings of the ego, there is some merit somewhere that has brought us to Amma. The Upanishads say that getting the Darshan of a Sad Guru is the beginning of our spiritual journey. Amma plays a most important role in making us realize that we are like the ever-effulgent sun, satchitānandam. Her nectarous words, whispered in our ears when we go for darshan, bring connectivity with our Self. Amma says that we must discriminate between what is real and what is unreal. This is because we are so immersed in this world and unable to recognize what is permanent and changing. This discrimination helps us see all things 'as they are' rather than what we think of them with our preconceived notions and concepts. Amma says that our real nature is unchanging. Everything that we perceive is impermanent. So one must do 'nethi,nethi.. vichāra,' that is, one must pursue a 'not this' line of thinking that negates the impermanent in our lives. This understanding awakens and strengthens our dispassion. We will no longer run after changing the world's changing objects and temptations. We will be able to hold our minds and senses centered in our higher Self without straying away from the spiritual path. Amma says an inquiry into our real nature brings us awareness. This will increase our aspiration to realize the real, which is the truth - the Self or Atman.

What is nethi, nethi vichār, or negation line of enquiry?

Amma says, If there exists a table, one may say 'this is my table,' but one will not say 'I am the table.' Similarly, if one has a car, one may say 'this is my car,' but one will not say 'I am the car.' Likewise, if one possesses an umbrella, one may say 'this is my umbrella,' but one will not say 'I am the umbrella.' Thus, in the same way, one needs to appreciate that all worldly things are not me.' About our body, one may often believe, 'I am the body,' so whatever happens to the body, we think it affects us. Instead, we should apply 'nethi.' ' I am not the body,' 'I am not mind and the thoughts, feelings and emotions that arise in it,' ' I am not ego,' ' I am not senses,' ' I am not prana,' ' I am not any of these,' 'nor their attributes am I,' 'neither the doer am I nor the agent am I.' Thus, we should discard all changing nature and realize that if I am not all these, then 'who am I?' This inquiry enables us to discover our real, permanent, unchanging, unborn, ever-free nature, which is 'Sat'.

Ambrosia

"Meditation is the ambrosia that makes you egoless and leads you to the state of no-mind. Once you transcend the mind, you cannot suffer. Meditation helps you to see everything as a delightful play so that all experiences, even the moment of death, can become blissful." -Amma

Amma's children are spread all around the globe. Most people who approach Amma seek answers to their pressing problems, either regarding their physical or mental health, life situations or spiritual progress. Amma shows us the way out of ignorance. While many find help to their pressing issues, she also gives us knowledge of our true nature, since all other knowledge is incomplete and will not provide permanence. These are all unreal. Amma says, 'Mind is samsāra (world),' 'which is sorrow.' Recognizing this fact is sadhana. We need to recognize that there is no happiness in the world. Only in our mind do we think that happiness exists somewhere else. On the contrary, Amma says 'you are the nature of happiness'-- 'tat twam asi (That Thou Art).' This is an age-old Upanishadic dictum also; indeed, eternal happiness is our real nature. Hence, we should discard attachments to names and forms. They will all fade and perish one day or the other. I look at the mirror to see my face. I don't look at the mirror to see the mirror! Thus, to know myself, I meet the Guru, hear the Upanishads, then realize that I am the 'seer' and also the essence of everything that is 'seen.'

The fundamental pattern visible in all living beings is the seeking of the favorable and the avoidance of all that which is unfavorable. However, the discerning mind quickly realizes that this pattern is almost constantly at odds with the ever-changing circumstances of life and thus brings one much suffering. When we understand the truth, we begin to pull back from indulging in this pair of opposites, realizing that these are anitya (impermanent). Our real nature is permanent, so we should discriminate to arrive at and to live this Truth. Fueling the mind and senses with the temporary objects of the world will only invite more suffering and bondage.

Amma represents Sanātana Dharma, which declares that Dharma, Artha, Kāma, and Moksha are the four aims of life. By dharma (righteous action), one should fulfill artha (wealth) and kāma (desires). By performing action based on dharma, our minds also slowly get purified. Then, when one hears and follows Guru's words, it leads to moksha (liberation). Thus, following dharma becomes a vital role that leads to our mind becoming content. With this clear mind, one should discriminate between what is beneficial and what is not, and pursue a life based on dharma.

We all carry much burden in terms of karma, and this cycle of birth and death will continue endlessly, until we take refuge in a Guru like Amma. Without such an influence, there is no escape from the world. We will forever continue the exhausting pattern of seeking the mirage of happiness in an ever-changing world that cannot give us what we seek. We desperately cling to people, objects, titles and wealth but in accordance with their nature, they will all leave us one day and cause much suffering to those attached to them. However, the Guru's love and compassion will heal the effects of our karmas. Through contact with a Guru like Amma, we enter the spiritual path and start walking the path of freedom.

However, there are also traps once we enter the spiritual path. We bring the same achievement mindset that we used in pursuing the pleasures and objects of the world to the spiritual path, and we start seeking spiritual experiences, spiritual powers, kundalini awakening, and so on. The venerable Adi Shankara says that all siddhis are equal to the droppings of a crow. It is also often seen that the so-called spiritual people become obsessed with the external displays of holiness. Sitting under a tree is not realization, nor is sitting on a mountain, in caves, or near river banks. We have to sit at the lotus feet of Sadguru Amma.

A Guru like Amma then starts to teach the disciple the eternal Truths, as expounded in the Upanishads. We should read or listen, reflect and contemplate these Truths until our conviction becomes firm. The cycle of Karma is endless and inevitably brings with it more experiences and births. However, when we realize this binding nature of Karma and perform our actions as an offering to the Guru, with awareness and maintain equanimity regarding the fruits of these actions, these actions do not bind us. This attitude of surrender to the Guru or Ishwara is Karma yoga.

As we proceed on the spiritual path, we begin to understand that whatever is seen is limited. So all our perceptions, feelings, sensations are limited. We exist in a world of limitations. This is called the disease of ignorance. If not diagnosed, it will lead us to ignorance more and more. The only thing that opposes and relieves this ignorance is knowledge, so we must seek knowledge that points to our real nature. Our real nature is the truth – Nitya (everlasting), suddha (ever-pure), buddha (conscious), muktha (ever-free). This knowledge is Satchidananda.

It is, indeed, not difficult for the Guru to give this knowledge to the disciple. The question is, "are we ready?" The qualified aspirant will genuinely benefit upon receiving this understanding. The Guru carefully instructs according to the disciple's maturity, so that knowledge will be fruitful. A qualified mind is purified by selfless service and devotion to Guru, vivēka (discrimination), vairāgya (detachment) and mumukshatva (burning desire to be free). With these noble traits, one develops the ability to realize their 'swarūpam' as 'Atma' when the Guru imparts knowledge. If we do not understand the Guru's words, it is then a sure recipe for us to be sacrificed at the altar of death.

We need this yearning to be free. We have to approach Amma. Then Amma will give us knowledge accordingly. If we keep quiet and say, 'Amma will do everything' or 'let Amma call me, then I will come to her,' these are all just lame excuses. It is only our laziness masquerading as surrender to the Guru. At other times, we keep quiet because we believe in astrological predictions, etc and believe it is not the right time to make efforts on the spiritual path. While all vedic sciences have some merit, it is not everything. Stars are not everything! We need to make efforts and perform sadhana.

Our real nature is Sat-Chit-Ananda (Being-Awareness-Bliss). Let's not yield to weakness! We, the children of the Creator,

Ishwara Himself, have to wake up to the Guru and arise from all thoughts of ignorance. Let us make effort through sadhana as instructed and let our minds be at the lotus feet of Amma. Nobody can perish in this path if they give their hearts to the Guru. Hence, by grace, by devotion, we should hear Amma's upadēśam to complete our sadhana.

Amma says, 'you are the essence of Om;' 'Om is Brahman;' 'Om is source;' 'all sadhanas speak about om;' ' become worthy of this knowing at the feet of the Guru.' 'Surrendering at Guru's feet from where all manifestations arise, exist for a while and finally merge, where all sadhana culminates. This is the highest fortune, highest accomplishment everybody aspires for.

The all embracing Mother

"Just like the person does not change despite playing different roles, I am not just the reflection in the mirror but I am the illuming consciousness behind that reflection and the source of it." - Amma

There is no better time than now, for those of us who have had the fortune to be in the presence of Amma, who is like a lighthouse for us. Basking in that Self-illumination (Swayam jyotish), lets us arrive at the Truth, so that we never get lost in this myriad world of names and forms.

What is Amma's real mission?

All kinds of people come to Amma. Amma embraces all and Amma rejects none. She is like a flowing river. In an Indian river, we can often see some people bathing, some washing their clothes, some others performing their sandhya prayers, or leaving lamps into the flowing waters as worship. The river accepts all and treats them all the same.

We see many kinds of people coming to Amma - spiritual sadhaks, sanyasis, actors, directors, doctors, engineers, scientists, politicians, simple villagers and children. Amma accepts all, blesses them, feeds them, prays with them, and also teaches them to pray and meditate. She is like the flowing river that embraces all.

Once, during the North India tour of 2012, Amma finished the lunch stop and was getting back into the camper. At that time, one Brahmacharini was holding her bleeding finger to show Amma that she had a cut on her finger.

Amma walked to her and told me to get the dressing materials. When I did that, Amma cleaned the wound with spirit, and then applied an antibiotic ointment. Then she tied a bandage with all love and care.

Meanwhile, I was thinking about why the Brahmacharini showed Amma the wound! I would have directly taken care of it easily. Even when she showed Amma the wound, Amma could have also just told me to take care of it, etc. But NO, Amma was responding to the innocence of Brahmacharini, and without feeling any fatigue after the lunch stop, Amma patiently did the dressing.

That love, that concern was a teaching to me. Amma can bless in numerous ways, and that Brahmacharini was lucky indeed. In the same way, Amma takes care of our bleeding minds by embracing and cleaning us with the seeds of devotion. Then she applies the ointment of knowledge. Finally, she dresses the wounds so that afflictions of samsāra like desire, anger, greed, pride, etc keep away from us, thus allowing us to heal. From this Amma's compassionate gesture, I learnt that nothing is insignificant; we have to take care of fellow beings when they are in distress.

So, Amma knows the level which each person is at, and comes down to their level. We are often like this Brahmacharini. She never pushes someone away saying that their issues are too trivial, or their problems are endless. People bring all kinds of problems to Amma - like:

* What should I study as my major?
* Should my son go abroad for his higher studies?
* I need to find someone to marry my son or daughter
* My marriage is in trouble, and I am thinking of getting a divorce
* My business is in serious trouble
* I or someone in my family is sick with cancer

Amma hears such problems over and over, both in person and through many letters that people write to her.

If we were to listen to such problems, we might give up after helping 10 people or so, claiming that the problems of the people are endless. But Amma is not like that. Amma is infinite in nature and infinite in wisdom.

Amma's presence and knowledge are a great blessing to us. Once I watched an interview of Amma. Amma was talking about the famous Malayalam movie star Mohan Lal. Amma said - "Lal mon has been coming to Amma since he was studying in college. He was very interested in meditation and spirituality. His belief in the immense inherent potential of a human being and his capacity to think meditatively - could have been the reason behind his ability to act fully absorbed in multifarious roles.

"Just like the person does not change despite playing different roles, I am not just the reflection in the mirror but I am the illuming consciousness behind that reflection and the source of it."

"Let Grace give this awareness to Lal-mon and also increase his strength to play the role of many more characters."

What a spontaneous flow of grace!

We have seen many doctors, scientists, engineers and many other people who have sacrificed all and have come to Amma's ashram. Many others, although continuing their lives amidst society, do whatever they can to contribute to Amma's mission and its activities, be it financially or through other ways. Amma has also enabled these people to use their talents for the benefit of society and has established super-speciality hospitals, universities, research labs, and so on. Just like Amma blessed Mohan Lal, similarly, the people who have sacrificed all, and their families who are living here at the ashram, and outside, irrespective of the roles they play here or outside are guided by Amma. Her ultimate purpose is to help them understand their unchanging Self-nature. The seva activities help them attain chitta shuddhi(purity of mind), forgiveness, patience, and so on, as well as serve humanity through their inventions and innovations.

It was on the battlefield of Kurukshetra, that Krishna imparted the wisdom of the Bhagavad Gita. There was no time for it then, but still, that was where this profound instruction happened. Where we are today, the times we live in, is another Kurukshetra. We are experiencing the chaos of the world around us, yet here is where we are to find peace. Arjuna surrendered to Sri Krishna, and the instruction of the Gita happened. Similarly, we have surrendered and have come to Amma. In turn, Amma is imparting eternal wisdom to us. Arjuna was a Kshatriya, his dharma was to fight and the battle could not be avoided. At the same time, irrespective of what one's role is externally in the world, it does not stand in the way of realizing one's Self-nature.

No matter what our role is in the external world, we are to use it as the means to develop divine qualities and to realize our Self-nature, just like Arjuna, despite being a warrior on the battlefield, realized his Self-nature and achieved contentment (Krtākrta).

Amma is operating in the same way, using all of the activities of her mission, as a medium to enable us to discover our Self-nature. We need these roles and activities to be the medium, because this is what our minds are completely immersed in. Just like a child, who clings to a doll, or like a 6-7 year old boy attached to his small bike, discards it for a bigger bike as a teenager, and later as a grown-up abandons that in favor of a motorcycle or a car.

Unlike today, where one might hang clothes on a rope, use clips to hold them in place and so on, during olden times, people would dry their clothes on plants, which may have thorns, etc to hold the clothes in place. Upon drying, one would not just yank the clothes off the plant from being torn. One needs to be careful.

Similarly, when we are fully identified with our external roles, it is difficult for us to discard them suddenly. If we try to abandon them all at once, and say "I'm going to renounce," it will lead to more problems. We might find ourselves stranded in the middle, neither here nor there. So we need to use the current roles, occupation, stage of life that we are in to imbibe spiritual principles and slowly move forward.

Amma has been at the forefront in providing assistance during various natural disasters, like the Tsunami, Gujarat earthquake, floods in Bombay, Surat or Uttarakhand, and so on. In addition to her naturally flowing compassion, she utilizes these dire situations to teach her children to practice love, compassion and serve. She sent us as doctors and nurses for caring and counseling the sick. The Brahmacharis built houses, toilets. These actions help the society, as well as the sevites. This is her intention.

Just like biking to work helps save money and also keeps you fit - Amma's mission in addition to multitude of charitable activities, imbibes spiritual qualities in her children, lightening their mind's load and helps them realize their Self-nature.

Amma says, even a tiny screw is important on an airplane. Without it, there could potentially be serious problems with an airplane. In the same way, nothing is wasted in Amma's world, everything is recycled. Everything is used to move forward. One may think they have no skills, but Amma uses them somehow, to serve the world. Amma encourages us to serve in whatever capacity we can. By this service we are in an eternal embrace of her infinite love and compassion.

In this way, Amma, the river of love and compassion awakes us to our true nature, even while we become instruments in her hands to serve the world as she sees fit. To bask in her presence, to experience her grace and to awaken to ourselves, what greater blessing can one ask for?

Amma the inexhaustible flame!

Everyone seeks the experience of never ending happiness. This is what everyone thirsts for. With this desire, the people of the world strive hard, take all kinds of risks, with the feeling that through such struggle and striving, they can achieve anything they put their minds to.

In the process of striving to satisfy their egotistical desires, humans no longer hesitate to grab what they want at the cost of the well-being of their fellow humans or nature. With no concern for the right attitude, greed drives one to go after the objects of their pursuit. Due to this mindset, human history is filled with tales of conflict, wars and destruction of nature. We are now at a point where humans themselves are affected, and have brought the downfall of the human race to their doorstep, and it is uncertain if humans can recover from it.

How is one to free oneself from such a situation? The first step is to see all the destruction that one has brought upon oneself and to everyone around us through selfishness. It is high time for us to change our egoistic thinking. If we cannot go beyond this, then death is inevitable. But, before humans perish miserably, is there a way out or release from all these confusions one has brought upon oneself and upon the world?

We need to learn together to see things 'as they are.' There is more to life than going from one situation or problem to the next. This does not mean we do not take care of things, people or issues as they arise. Minor problems day to day are inevitable. For example - If we own a car, we have to fill gas and do all the necessary maintenance work as needed. The same will apply to all our needs. As the need arises, we get things. Still, life is not all about the need itself. Yes, we have to attend to them, starting from our body, mind along with all those who depend on us. That doesn't mean life is only maintenance work. Don't you think so? Deep in our hearts, we have to know that life unfolds every situation according to our prarabdha karma. Still, when we contemplate deeply, we will understand that life is not all situation-based.

Without questioning such deep rooted concepts and beliefs we hold regarding the world, relationships, objects, power, wealth, etc, we will never improve in knowing our way out of these beliefs. Do we want to hold on to all that we have learned, this erroneous belief system that has caused us much suffering and is highly questionable? If one is serious about being free, then the first step to take on the path to Truth and freedom is to question our deeply held beliefs regarding the world and how we approach and interpret events and experiences.

All objective experiences change all the time. When we try to hold on to it, it leaves us in despair. Then why don't we try to learn from all these day-to-day experiences? If we examine it properly, then we will know that they are all temporary. 'What has come will go.' If we truly understand this, we will not pursue that which will disappoint us in the end. We will desire to know something endless, in turn, which is birthless so that it will be everlasting, ancient, eternal, which is completeness itself. To realize this alone is the purpose of one's birth. Otherwise, one will be chasing mirages only for the rest of his life; for no reason, one has to pay a tax of suffering. We just waste our life, not realizing it to be precious like diamonds; we believe it is a plain stone and throw it away. Awakening won't happen unless we go to mahatmas humbly, seek their blessing by doing service, and hear their Truth. It is not their imagination; it is the truth of Upanishads they put in simple words for us to realize.

How come one is not getting help? Why does one have to suffer?

We often hear the people of the world exclaim as above. Frankly, it is just an excuse to say that. Saints have taken birth since time immemorial. Even today a Satguru, like Amma lives, providing solace to the suffering ones. Such beings give life to all scriptures, teaching which Sanatana dharma has given us, bringing peace to light, and providing all needed in one's life. So we need to ask ourselves, are we really serious about knowing, realizing the truth, or do we ask these questions out of just a casual curiosity?

Amma says 'creator and creation are not different.' 'It is one only' 'like water and waves, gold and ornaments.'

To understand this, we have to give a place for the creator who has created this creation. Hence, enquiry into this creator is important. If we ask 'why has he created it?' Then the Srutis say - 'that it is his nature to do so' 'not only that he has created but also entered and pervaded it without leaving any gap.' This means he is filled by himself in and out, through and through he alone is. The rest is the appearance of himself in variety. The experience of that Ishwara, who is first and foremost in everything, is seen in the seers like Amma. Whatever they do will be the offering to Ishwara. This is because they have realized the oneness with Ishwara, the very Atma --The inner Self, the Brahman, the non-dual pure Awareness. They have realized that oneness, so they are revered. Hence, their company is the only way out of this samsāra - this bondage of ignorance. This is the experience of the ancient rishis, which now Amma stands for. This is the Guru parampara, the eternal light of Sanatana dharma.

As we said, Ishwara has created this world and is very much alive in this creation. It is through his eyes, we see, through his energy, we are alive. Through his all-knowingness, we can experience this creation of beauty. His help is there all the time. That is why we are breathing. That is why we get water to drink. He created plants for our food. When we understand this omnipresence of Ishwara, we should be filled with humility and gratitude. Thus, we should cultivate the feeling of the presence of the omnipresent Ishwara everywhere, in everything, including ourselves. By nurturing this attitude to see the greatness of Ishwara in everything, to feel gratitude and to be loving, compassionate, caring in our interactions with nature and our fellow beings.

So as we feel the burden of suffering, caused due to our own ignorant actions, and strive towards freedom and to realize Truth, Amma comes to us. She is there for our help to all who feel lost, despair, not knowing what to do, facing turmoil all the time. "The All-compassionate Ishwara in the form of sadguru Amma without any expectation, full of love and compassion incarnated where she walks into our lives to make us realize the true nature of ours. Satchidananda."

What is that Amma is doing, why Amma is giving darshan day and night?

It is not easy to understand Amma as the mind is overpowered by ego, so all have been deluded. It is the Guru's tremendous patience and sacrifice that brings one to realize the Truth. For Amma, it is not difficult; as Amma says, 'love has no tiredness and otherness.' She is revamping the society's whole system through her embrace, which is the highest Truth that one has never seen before or will see in the future.

The embrace is the bond of Consciousness, the bond of divinity, the bond of trust, and the bond of love, which can never break as it is the one. Which is eternal, which Amma stands for. All illusion of separation ends, culminating in wholeness.

It is day and night for us, but for Amma, like the sun, which never sees day or night and is ever effulgent. She works tirelessly for her children, where all the human limitations do not apply. All we have to do is come to her presence. Beyond that, she will take over in that eternal embrace. If one is serious in knowing the truth, Amma makes them understand that she is not separate from us. In her all-embracing love that is the Truth. The boats flow easily in the direction of the river current. Similarly, the current of Amma's embrace carries us across the delusions of life and death. The ego just has to stop its illusionary tricks. This feeling of the mother, Guru, companion, friend, and all relation we seek in the world culminates in her divinity, where sacredness is only left without any traces of ego. All Hearts are open to her. Nothing is left to hold us to this world of conflicts. She has absorbed all.

Why then are people still confused, when there is no place for it? Very subtle understanding is necessary. Amma works for all her children to awaken them no matter what she has to undergo. She has given herself entirely for the needy ones. Whoever wants her help, after realizing that all worldly attachments and pleasures can never bring Truth or happiness, can stay with her to get guidance.

Why do we have to listen to her?

Amma speaks words of Sruti, which are Upanishads. Through her natural state spontaneously by her very presence, touch, smile, and compassionate look, Her love, which is healing, reveals the highest Truth. To hold on to Amma, we should develop the vivēka, which is discrimination of real and unreal, as all our experiences are changing. Next, we should build dispassion as nothing can give everlasting experience, so all objects of desire prevent us from knowing the truth, then sit at the lotus feet of Amma and listen to her.

'All this interest in worldly things and its business is like catching a crocodile mistaking it for the wood log to cross the river. Nothing we brought with us, alas nothing we will take when we depart. Why get so deluded with this only temporary wealth? Take what is necessary, as that is not your goal. Why do you go after name and fame? Everybody only respects you for some time, as long as you are taking care of them by some means. When wealth is gone or when you are diseased, nobody will be there. This thirst to experience them is foolish. They all, in some way or another, will leave us dejected in no time. With discriminative thinking and leaving them when it becomes an obstacle to know the Truth,' this Amma sings in her bhajans for all common people to understand. She awakens us from our long slumber of ignorance.

In conclusion, We should keep Amma in front. Then she will become the beacon of our lives. Guiding us safely from these illusions of life by removing the ignorance from our hearts makes us realize oneness with her.

Amma's smile

"Once you are able to see the Truth, nothing is unknown or strange to you; you are familiar with the entire universe and you smile, not occasionally, but continuously. Your life becomes a big smile." – Amma

When Mahatmas, like Amma, smile, they communicate the most subtle aspects of the reality of our Self. We usually think that a smile is when our facial muscles do a little exercise while we pose for our selfies to post on social media. But Amma's Smile has a more profound sense. It's a smile with an insight telling others too to smile.

We live by identifying ourselves with our name, body, mind, and various other labels all our lives. The world says, 'you are so and so.' Human beings then embrace these face labels on themselves and suffer unnecessarily. This false identity is what the Mahatmas smile at. They smile at and tell others to recognize the Truth and smile at all this false belief. We are not these fictional notions because our Self is infinite, immortal. It is existence, awareness, and bliss, ever free of suffering. The smile of Amma shows that one's real nature is ever free but is misunderstood to be bound because of māya.

In this identification with the body, mind, senses, intellect, and world, some cry, some laugh. Happiness and misery are a misnomer. It is a joke to believe that samsāra belongs to oneself. Mahatmas smile, seeing the plight of the individuals.

Some think they are sinners and go on pilgrimages, take a dip in holy rivers, and give charity. But when they really examine themselves, they find that their plight is the same, with bondage and misery in their hearts.

Some others observe spiritual practices and read the scriptures hoping that one fine day they will be free. But ignorance does not leave them. They feel desperate. Seeing this, Mahatmas like Amma smile.

The Upanishadic teaching purports to point out that 'you are That. That is the Awareness, what one Self is; there is no one in bondage to strive for liberation; one's reality is ever free Self.'

Elaborating on the point, the Upanishads give an anecdote:

Once a boy went to a place where he saw his reflection in a mirror and started crying because his reflected face was distorted with dirt. He identified himself with the defective reflection of his face. He started cleaning his face, but the reflection could not be rectified. He was deluded that his face was distorted with dirt.

Noticing the crying boy, a passer-by came to the boy and asked, 'what happened?' The boy said that his face was distorted with dirt on it. He could not get rid of the dirt despite washing his face again and again. The mirror showed the same dirty distorted face.

Seeing the boy's lack of discrimination and suffering, the passer-by first smiled. Then, he came to the boy, took compassion, and patiently explained to the boy that whatever dirt was on the face in the reflection did not affect his real face. Whatever he saw was due to the defective surface of the mirror. Due to identification with the reflection, he is crying without any reason. He told the boy that because of the defect in the mirror, his method of getting rid of the defect, such as cleaning the face, did not help the boy.

Hearing these words, the boy realized that his face was ever clean without any distortion or dirt, though it appeared so in the mirror. With this understanding again, he saw the reflection in the mirror. Furthermore, it appeared with the same distortion and dirt, but this time he smiled!

The boy's face is 'Atma.' The mirror is the mind where one gets identified with the body-mind-world. Reflection is 'individual jīva' or 'separate self' (reflected face) or 'identified self' with body, mind, senses, intellect, and world.

The crying of the boy refers to the 'lack of discrimination.' Because of that, one thinks he is bound to this ocean of transmigration and feels 'I am happy,' 'I am miserable' with the notions of doership and enjoyership

The Passer-by here is the Guru or knower of truth. Seeing our confusion, Mahatmas like Amma, smile and take compassion on the aspirant who surrenders at his lotus feet.

The aspirant, not knowing how to be free of samsāra with the misidentification of himself, faces innumerable experiences of sorrow and happiness that come to the Guru's feet. Like Krishna smiled, seeing Arjuna in a desperate and crying mood before the war, and with compassion taught Arjuna the reality regarding Self.

The one who developed the notion that 'I am the body' and 'whatever happens to the body is happening to me' feels next that 'I am the mind.' Consequently, he either suffers or feels happy going with the various moods of the mind. He thinks it is his problem, likewise identifying himself with the intellect, senses, and the world. He suffers because there is a lack of discrimination. He fails to discern between the real Self and identified self. This ignorance is the cause of suffering. The Guru, with a smile, teaches the Truth to the aspirant.

Teachings: The 'Upanishads say that the Self (Atma) gets identified with the mind as it is proximate to it.'

The identified self or reflected consciousness is called by the name jīva, the individual Self. In Truth, the individual self is an appearance in Awareness.

'With the identification with the body, mind, senses, intellect, and world, the individual self suffers the consequences of actions it does with the notion of being an agent as doer and enjoyer of the experiences of happiness or misery.'

'It is only 'as if' the Self appears as an individual self due to identification. That is why it is called māya or illusion because, without any reason, he identifies with the unreal world. The individual Self does not have an existence of its own. In the light of Awareness, all the individual 'selves' appear to have existence. Due to his ignorance, one thinks oneself to be the body, mind, senses, intellect, and world.'

'Thus, the jīva gets exhausted in his ignorance, suffering without freedom. He cries with the agony for freedom but fails to get it.'

'Thinking oneself to be a sinner, he associates with religious works by going around sacred places and taking holy dips in all rivers, Then chanting the names of various gods and practicing meritorious actions like giving charity and serving the sick. But the ignorance deep in the heart is not removed.

All good works and other spiritual practices like japa, chanting and meditation bring about the purification of the heart and one-pointedness to mind. So one takes refuge in Guru to hear the wisdom of truth so that his ignorance is removed. Because only knowledge regarding the reality of Self as non-doer of any act can destroy the results of work by eliminating false ignorance caused due to false identifications, thus realizing of the Self dawns without any doubt.'

'In reality, the Self never became bound with identifying the unreal nature of the body-mind-world complex. Ever free, ever-existent, ever aware and ever blissful.'

'Never was their bondage nor a need for freedom for the Self.' With this wisdom of seeing how the jīva suffers without any reason comes the smile.

The necessity of knowledge, a Guru and his teachings for an aspirant arises because of identification with indescribable nescience, which brought samsāra to the jīva. Knowledge makes the aspirant aware of the Self, which is ever free of the unawareness.

Conclusion: Amma's smile is the smile of knowledge where ignorance has no place. It is like the light where darkness has no place. Whatever other methods are used for removing the darkness fails as ignorance is not a thing or object.

Amma sees all these and smiles as all that is needed is for us to gain the correct knowledge regarding the nature of our Self.

She tells others to smile and know that there was never bondage for one to get liberated from as one is in reality already ever-free, ever-pure, ever-existent, ever-aware, ever-blissful. Amma's smiles with compassion looking at our foolish, helpless plight. It is like our smile seeing a child's unnecessary restlessness, foolish behavior, and helplessness. Then the mother hugs and instructs the child the truth about how to tackle the situation.

'Amma's smile is from the eye of infinite wisdom.'

'That's why Amma's eyes glitter with the brilliance of thousands of suns and even more as she has the eye of infinity.'

'When Amma says smile, we should get that eye of knowledge and not just make a smiley face for a Facebook selfie.'

That's why Mahatmas like Amma say:

'Smile at death before it laughs at you.' 'Amma's smile is the inexhaustible flame of knowledge.'

See everything from the self standpoint

Atmavil kude vyaktiya kananam (See everything from the Self standpoint) and not otherwise! - Amma

प्रतिबोधविदितं
Pratibodhaviditam
- Kena Upanishad 2-4
Awareness is known when it is recognized as the indwelling-Self in each modification (arising in the mind).

यत्साक्षादपरोक्षाद्ब्रह्म, य आत्मा सर्वान्तरः
yatsākṣādaparokṣādbrahma, ya ātmā sarvāntarah
- Brihadaranyaka Upanishad3-4-1
That Awareness is direct and immediate
is the Self indwelling in all.

सदेव सोम्येदमग्र आसीदेकमेवाद्वितीयम् ।
Sad ēva soumya idam agra āsid ekam evādvitīyam
- Chandogya Upanishad 6-2-1
There was Existence alone in the beginning,
one only, without a second.

Introduction

Amma says, 'all the way through, see every being as one's Self-modulating in all appearances and not the other way as nonself.' The Guru, speaking from that samyak drishti - right vision viewpoints, is samyak jñāna, i.e., right knowledge, which is the highest Upanishad, the words of the Śruti.

Self is the witness and not different from the witnessed. Atma dristi is only real drsti. All other drishti are anatma drishti, which is samsāra. Those who are caught in samsāra move from bondage to bondage, never getting to the essence. The real Advaita expresses naturally in Amma through her embrace and touch and in her soothing words of wisdom. It is like light revealing light wherever it shines because light cannot be anything other than light. Amma sees herself in millions of people whom Amma meets personally. From that ocean of Awareness, Amma is the manifest grace that has come to us to awaken us to this truth.

Recognizing the Self

When we see space between two objects, space between two words, space between two thoughts, slowly, it is understood that space is the one which is always seen first, followed by objects, words, and thoughts. Hence, everything arises in space, exists in space, and finally merges in space, just like a screen is a backdrop for all images. Or like all images that appear on a television screen. Or like the pixels seem as all images on a computer monitor. The Self cannot appear as other than Awareness. It is the very nature of oneself. It is immediate. It is the one that is available in every thought, sensation, and perception. Within and without, all beings are made only of Awareness and are illuminated by Awareness. Thus, inevitably Awareness is one, which is unchanging. We can perceive It; otherwise, it would not have been possible. It is the very proof of I -the inner Self (Pratyagātma) -the indwelling Self whom everybody addresses concerning everything. Self is immediate, first and foremost; all the rest are indeed its variegated modifications. By seeing the undivided Awareness as the very backdrop, one will know that Awareness is enlivening everything. Revealing itself in waking and dream states various appearances, and in a deep sleep, 'it is as it is.'

In all our thoughts, sensations, perceptions, it is Awareness revealing Awareness. Therefore, everything arises, sustains, merges in Awareness, as one, unless the Śruti or the Guru points out this truth, is not recognized.

Sadhana required

Through the exercise of discrimination, this becomes clear. We can clear it only by removing the obstacle of ignorance, concepts and imagination regarding Awareness. The very nature of the thing is known when 'what is not' is negated. By negating various names and forms, the gold is revealed. Thus a negation of otherness like body, mind, senses, and world complex the very Awareness is revealed. In other words, the Self is ever free of all limitations superimposed on it.

Here we are not inferring Self like how we assume it is windy by seeing the movement of leaves in a tree. We are neither keeping mind in stillness to realize the Self. Or they are keeping mind in someplace like going into samādhi state, or trying to stop the inputs like all triggering factors required for our day-to-day activities. Hence, all happening, sharing, experiencing is not appearing in the mind like an individual. The very mind appears in one continuous background of Awareness, which is Self-illumined as all are its modulations. Waves rise and fall, but water, as such, is not disturbed. The mind's real nature is Awareness. Wherever all the thoughts, sensations, perceptions are experienced as Awareness 'that I am,' this is the real atma drišti. It is a very natural Being and a state of ease with all. In other words, it is the very nature of everything; Awareness is never veiled, like how the clouds cannot cover the sun. Hence, from the standpoint of Awareness, the mind is no problem; all are only appearances in imagination. Indeed, no imagination can affect Awareness, which is ever free. So here, the right perspective or samāyak jñāna is needed and must be nurtured. This nurturing of our identification with Awareness, as the Being that by its very nature sees the ever modifications of the mind and world, without becoming identified and responding to each thought through the limited personality's preferences of like and dislike. This indeed is sadhana, and when this becomes effortness, it is also the goal.

Presence

The presence of Amma is most powerful. In that divine flow, all get embraced. In every movement of Amma, Awareness is revealed. Her presence is unaffected by happiness or sorrow. Since the nature of the self is happiness in nature and since everybody desires happiness, everyone is drawn to her presence. In all actions, Amma makes us understand the reality of the Self, and all are embraced in that presence of Amma.

At the same time, her powerful presence is also a mirror which enables us to know our nature. When We see our face in the mirror, we correct all the defects similarly in that presence, all our negative tendencies are exposed and corrected. Amma waits patiently for us to evolve. Amma sees the Self in all and there is no 'otherness' or differentiation. Hence, our ignorance should go away. We should discriminate and arrive at the truth. We should recognize the subtle aspect of our attachments and renounce them, even the attachment to be in the presence of Amma.

When we stand free from all attachments and identifications to false labels, we realize our true nature as the substratum in which the world appears, exists and subsides. To realize and exist as this is perennial happiness. Amma's presence brings about this viewpoint, i.e., Atma driśti.

Conclusion

'Let us sit at the Holy Lotus feet of the master, and arrive at the right understanding, by clearing our doubts and eliminating all wrong concepts we currently possess regarding ourselves and the world. Then alone, Atma Driśti, the very nature, is realized as an expression of everything.'

'With Amma's blessings, we have been brought to her presence, no matter the posture of the relationship we approach her with - be it madness, friendship, hatredness, surrender with devotion, guru-disciple relationship, mother- child relationship or just to receive the benefit of being around her. Amma accepts us as we are, and Amma patiently will work on us and help us realize our Sat nature which is there before creation and even now behind all of these self-imposed identities we embrace. Amma remembers all our past, that is why her love and compassion has no selfish motives and is beyond all reason. Let us just surrender at the lotus feet and move forward, then the benediction of peace, love, Sat is realized as infinite reality, where there is no individual seeking self. Instead immortal Awareness is one's real Self and it is the Self of everything without any differences.'

Atmaswarūpam and premaswarūpam thou art

"Children, Your happiness is Mother's health. Mother has no health other than that." Therefore, children, do selfless service and spiritual practice, without wasting time – and attain real bliss. Your time is precious, so move cautiously, with awareness, towards your goal: Truth, Consciousness and Bliss." -Amma

(Note; write up is based on Anubhava, Sruti, Yukthi)

Introduction

On coming to receive Amma's darshan, everyone has an experience. But once they return to their normal daily lives, filled with mundane activities, this experience appears to get covered up. Then one feels as if it is lost. In reality, it can never be lost, since what Amma does is to plant spiritual seeds in one's heart.

However, this feeling of losing the special experience of being in Amma's arms after a while is due to the worldly samskāras or tendencies in our minds, that overpower the pure experience of being in Amma's presence.

So what spiritual practices can one perform, in order to retain or further strengthen Amma's presence with us? One needs to develop a meditative mind, dedicate one's actions to her, and develop vivēka and Vairāgya (discrimination and dispassion). Then, one should hear the Amma's upadēśa, which are Śruti words, which point out our real nature. Furthermore, we must then develop a conviction in the 'real–sat' nature which was pointed to by Amma. So, one should not stop his sadhana. Instead, one has to continue.

Simultaneously, one has to help their intellect also get a conviction in one's Atmaswarūpam (Self nature). So, Shravana (listening to amma's words), then Manana (to get rid of doubts in words of Amma & one's real nature by Śruti-Yukhti help). Then Nididhyāsana – to eliminate all thoughts, which makes one think 'I am the body-mind complex.' So, all this sadhana finally culminates in Atma jñāna (Self-knowledge).

Anubhava

"The master destroys obstacles and reveals to the seeker the sacred path." -Amma

Amma is a great fountain of uncolored Love and Compassion bound by no strings. She does not cater to any one particular group or only to a lucky few. She encompasses the entire universe as her mind. In her all-embracing nature, Amma understands the suffering of humanity – suffering that she sees caused due to a finite mind stuck in a miserable state. The limited human-made mind suffers in various ways, fluctuating with the ups and downs of joy, despair, anxiety, fear, pleasure, conflict in relationships, etc. There seems to be no end to these experiences where we are tossed from one situation to another, day in and day out.

Amma's love and compassion heals

"To lovingly caress people, console and wipe their tears, until the end of this mortal frame is Amma's wish. Amma bows down to all of you, whose true nature is pure love and supreme consciousness." -Amma

Our efforts to understand the nature of the mind will be limited because we are already traumatized. Any amount of adjustments we make in our life are crippled even before we start. So Amma plays a vital role in helping us overcome our life situations, and to understand and effectively regain our true nature.

Only Love with compassion can understand what chaos the mind has brought to the world, including the wars. Healing has to happen in our lives. Love is universal. It does not belong to anyone or only the privileged. Anybody can access what Amma stands for. Amma is universal. This is what Amma points to us in her embrace. She does this by removing the obstacles to the flow of love by moving from being a personal 'me' to being universal.

All so-called obstacles are our worldly knowledge, achievements, despair, anxiety, fragmented thinking, tendency of seeking pleasure, failure to achieve, anger, loss, survival, struggle, etc. These are the kinds of problems we identify ourselves with. Amma points to love and compassion, which are already there within us but unnoticed. Spontaneously Amma radiates love in every word, through her eyes, through her being. Seeing this clearly will end the personal burden and find the current of love as one's intrinsic nature, bringing about healing.

Love and Compassion do not vary from man to man, whatever be the nationality. So a sense of complete peace and acceptance is felt in her presence. Her embrace is tender and full of affection. Seeing each one's feelings in their hearts and minds relieves the pain, feelings of hurt, etc. Her attention is immense, and that becomes the solution to their problems. Amma is free from all conditioning. In that freedom comes action, which is intelligence in its very nature. She sings the tune of love and compassion into one's soul, and its ecstasy has no boundaries. This is the experience of millions who have turned to her presence. It is the rare treasure they cherish, which they carry for many lives, if they are born again!

Amma's darshan

"What Amma does is not work. It is worship... Amma is worshiping her children as God. Children, you are all Amma's God." -*Amma*

Amma embraces the whole being when we go to her darshan. Conflicts are consumed in the fire of her embrace. No two entities remain then. It is one universal being that remains. Refreshed now, the power of love and compassion takes over. Her darshan speaks itself, and it is Meditation, freedom, and remaining in oneself. It is very special because we are not different from Amma. She is a universal mother, and we belong to her. This feeling of amma awakens in us. This is the truth where our small limited mind stops putting on the mask of separation, which brings the conflict in us.

When we meet a person for the first time, we usually note the gender, overall looks, amiability, professional expertise, social status, etc. We tend to judge the person from the angle of their usefulness for ourselves. Thus our assessment of accepting a relationship depends on their physical body, appearance, mental traits, and how far they will serve our purpose.

In contrast, when we go for darshan, Amma sees our Premaswarūpam, Atmaswarūpam. She immediately connects with us paying no attention to our shortcomings, emotions, or conflicts.

She joins us with her bond of love and compassion and acknowledges our need to come to her, i.e., whatever has brought us to her. The antaryāmi in our hearts, the inner Ishwara, the Lord that connects us with Amma. So, this happens in a fraction of a second unnoticed by us. Our heart melts in her presence. Our mind settles in silence in her embrace. When a new dimension opens up in us, revealing our true nature Atmaswarūpam, premaswarūpam, as Amma says. Her darshan will awaken the samskāra of love and compassion in us. Amma nourishes our being to make us strong.

Amma's presence is meditation

"Mahatmas can bestow a blessing, which even God cannot. God is nameless and formless; He cannot be seen. Mahatmas give reality to the existence of God and bless people with a tangible experience of Him. In their presence, people can see, feel and experience God. They perform the greatest renunciation of all; leaving the Supreme Abode of Bliss to live in the midst of ordinary people, like one of them, while remaining in eternal union." -Amma

When Amma listens completely to our problems, the gap between Amma and us comes to an end. When we see endless human problems, we have to give them full attention without resistance. Then, it is Meditation. There is a silence in that.

What is bringing us close to our real nature is Amma. Suffering does not belong to you or me. The way out is to see this with all our being. Love and compassion is the communication bridge that Amma uses because words fall short of pointing out that truth to oneself. This love is free from the burden of knowledge. The freedom born from there expresses the action with great intelligence and a concern for fellow human beings. That very care is healing humanity. With that sensitivity, whatever Amma does, a new creation unfolds with great beauty, as there is no expectation from anything.

What is that we see in Amma as unique. It is a continuous expression of an innocent flow, a sacredness, a divinity that is unblemished. The tremendous energy of compassion touching one's heart is a blessing. It is immeasurable and completely absorbs you. One has to see this seriously, and out of that comes the action, dropping the little me. In that very negating of little me, one finds the ground of Amma, which was there all the time but unnoticed. The breathing eases. This space is very important to recognize and stay with it. This is an awareness that is our inherent nature. Just staying effortlessly with great intelligence and without condemnation or justification means there is no me. It is consumed in the love of Amma. Separation means one is an individual who is born and will die miserably. Still, if he sees the futility of all these, he will be out of this confusion. A meditative mind is needed for everything, which means seeing all suffering arising from all images of me and then entering into Meditation. Such a way of seeing spreads the perfume in all our activities. That freedom is peace in the true sense. Amma is established in Brahman, and she sees us from that standpoint only. So everything is Atmaswarūpam, premaswarūpam for Amma. We need her presence more and more like plants need the sunlight to grow. We have to utilize her presence, observing all the sādhanas as instructed. This is noticed in the presence of Amma by itself and is Meditation.

Śruti:
'Amma's upadēśa IS Śruti '

"Whatever a Self-realized soul does holds a message that conveys the deeper principles of life." -Amma

Amma's upadēśa is complete. After tuning to her presence, one has to do further to intensify all sādhanas one is doing.

i.e., to get conviction, fulfillment, and realize the oneness with Amma. We have to be careful not to stop our sādhana but to persevere in this path to get the knowledge of what Amma wants us to realize. Amma tells us to know the nature of Real (Atma) and the unreal (Atma). 'The unreal is impermanent and changing by nature.' 'The Real is our true swarūpam' so, "Atmaswarūpam thou art, Premaswarūpam thou art." The meaning of this, we get only from the śruti of the Upanishad words 'tat twam asi.' An analysis is needed here.

Amma says, 'Atmaswarūpam thou art, Premaswarūpam thou art,' it is parama pramāńa (ultimate statement or authority). There is nothing to contradict this, as the Upanishad itself says so. Whatever is uttered by one established in Brahman, the Self, will be the final words. Each statement is filled with the revelation of Consciousness – in words emanating from such 'brahmaniśth' to reach that conclusion culminating in Brahma jñānam, i.e., realizing our true nature (Atma) by hearing their words of truth.

Yukthi : We will now analyze slowly to arrive at this truth (Amma's upadēśam is Śruti) by trying to understand the nature of Atma (Self) and the nature of anātma (non-Self)

The nature of sat (Atma) or Self – This is That which never changes.

The nature of asat (Anātma) or the unreal non-Self - always changing, impermanent, that which comes and goes (Āgamapiya). Other words for asat are Prakriti, mithya, māya, ajñānam.

Here we are not saying that the world's unreal nature is non-existent like the horns of a rabbit, a barren woman's son, or a sky flower. These are called atyantaabhava – nonexistent.

We experience the world, but at the same time, we understand that it is not altogether real because it was not there before creation and will not be there after destruction. So it appears only in between, Let's talk about a pot as an example - it was clay before its creation and will be clay after destruction, the "pot" only appears in the middle. Upon analysis, one finds all objects in creation to be similar, and to be of an impermanent nature.

So the world is not sat. So it is not real or non-existent. It is different from these, so it is indescribable (anirvacanīyam).

If we examine the nature of each object in this world starting from our bodies, we will understand its nature in detail.

"Forgetting the soul and worshiping the body is like ignoring electricity and believing that the electrical equipment runs on its own." -Amma

BODY: It is born, undergoes various stages of life - youth, adulthood, middle age, old age, then it finally dies. Then in between, it becomes fat, thin, tall, short, healthy, sick and so on. So this body has a beginning, continually changed and then it ends - hence its nature is impermanent, changing.

MIND: Sankalpa and vikalpa (decision and indecision) is its very nature - we continuously experience this nature of the mind which endlessly undergoes transformations. Each thought arises from silence and merges back into silence, and a new one emerges. Thus, the nature of the mind is also impermanent and ever changing.

PRĀNA: The nature of Prāna, the life-force is to ever-flow. Its nature is hunger and thirst born from rajoguna of panćabhūtas (5 elements), so it is always active. When we experience hunger – we provide food to prana within our body. When thirsty, we provide water to it

SENSES: Eyes see, Ears hear, Tongue tastes, Nose smells, Skin feels sensations. Each has its function. We cannot interchange or extinguish any of these functions.

INTELLIGENCE: Decides, so it decides various things.

WORLD: Everything from subtle to gross changes, nobody can stop it.

Gita refers to all of the above as āgamapayah, i.e., they come and go or are anitya (transient)

In contrast to the above, the nature of Sat, which is Atma or the Self is Nitya –That means it exists in all three periods of time (past, present and future) and in all the states of the mind (waking, dreaming and sleep). This is our real nature as satchitānandam (Existence, Awareness, Bliss), Nitya: Everlasting, Shuddha: Ever Pure, Buddha: Awareness, Mukta: Ever Free

But what is happening is, we are superimposing them mutually, i.e., sat (Atma) on asat (anātma) and asat (anātma) on sat (Atma) and we go about our lives performing our day-to-day activities spontaneously with this superimposition. Even though Atma and Anātma are contradictory, like light and darkness, this mixing up happens without discrimination, and due to this, we suffer.

HOW? – How does this Superimposition (Adyāsa) occur?

Suppose something happens to the body (Anātma). In that case, we superimpose this on our Self (Atma) and we say things like, 'I was born, I am fat, I am thin, I am short, I am tall, I am sick, I am wounded,' etc

Similarly, suppose anything happens to mind (Anātma), we superimpose the state of the mind and its modifications on our Self (Atma) — and we say, ' I am sad, I am happy, I am angry, I am jealous, I am proud, I am hurt' etc....

In the world (Anātma), when we identify with the objects, we superimpose our Self (Atma) on them and say 'this is mine' or 'this is not mine' and then claim to be the owner, the doer or enjoyer, etc....and do our activities. Due to this identification, we suffer when these objects we believe to be 'mine' change in ways we do not like.

This superimposition occurs and continues endlessly because we constantly re-affirm the erroneous beliefs of taking the non-self to be the Self. From the moment the body comes into existence, one's parents and the society around us teaches us to believe ourselves to be the labels they assign to us. We are taught that the objects of the world are worth pursuing and the achievement and possession of them brings happiness. We see everyone around us engaged in these pursuits, and thus re-affirming each others' delusions, we engage in the never ending pursuit of seeking permanence in the impermanent. This illusion has existed from time immemorial and will last forever.

How can we get rid of this superimposition that we are entangled in, like a silkworm entangled in a cocoon and unable to come out?

Sadhana and eligibility

Without waiting for others to change, if we change ourselves first, that will make a difference. -Amma

Vivēka (Atma–anātma vivēka) - This is the discrimination between Real & Unreal. That is, placing everything (the world and its objects and our real nature) in its right place is discrimination. Through this discrimination, we are not changing the nature of the objects of the world. We are just placing everything in the right context, and seeing things as they are. For example - the nature of fire is heat and light, the nature of ice is cold. We do not seek to change the nature of things, but through discrimination, we only learn to stop assigning additional value to these objects.

Vairāgya

"Crying for God is far superior to crying for trivial and fleeting worldly pleasures. The happiness we get from the objects of the world lasts only for a few seconds; whereas the bliss we experience from remembering God is everlasting." -Amma

Renouncing the desire for objects of this world and other worlds or anything that is an obstacle in knowing our real nature is Vairāgyam.

Attachment to unreal (anātma) things will bring bondage, so taking only what is necessary and being content with that brings strength to listen to scriptures by keeping the focus on the goal.

Shama-dama-shadsampat

"True happiness comes from the dissolution of the mind, not from external objects. Through meditation, we can achieve everything, including bliss, health, strength, peace, intelligence and vitality." -Amma

Control of mind: Controlling the nature of the mind is to wander away aimlessly from our real nature

Control of senses: Controlling five senses to flow outwards to their respective objects

Endurance, Forbearance (titiksha): towards all dvandvas (pairs of the opposite), as they all come and go and are impermanent,

shraddha: In the words of Guru and Upanishads, so that we listen to them with our heart and realize what they say,

uparati: not going back to the objects once renounced, as it happens all the time if we don't have proper conviction in the truth,

Samādhāna: maintaining tranquility, so that anxiety, emotions, etc. will not take us away from shravaṅa.

Mumukshutva

"The agony caused by the longing to see God is not sorrow; it is bliss. The state that we attain by calling and crying to God is equal to the bliss that the yogi experiences in samādhi. To cry for God is not at all a mental weakness, but rather helps us to gain the highest bliss." -Amma

Mumukshutva means burning aspiration to get freedom from ignorance. So one seeks a Guru to guide him to realize the

Truth. So he dedicates his life to achieve this goal by serving the master and learning the scriptures.

shravaṅa –listening to gurus upadēśa;

Practicing all of the above-said sadhana. When we are listening to the words of Guru and Upanishads, it says, 'tat twamasi' 'Atmaswarūpam' 'Premaswrūpam'...By saying this, they are pointing to our 'sat' (Atma)–real nature because we are 'sat' by very nature,

abāditajñāna (unsublated knowledge);

There is no other jñāna to replace or sublate this jñāna of our real nature (Atma) as we are that always. So it is called abāditajñāna (unsublated knowledge). Upanishad has no other word to negate 'tat twamasi,' so it is called paramapramāṅa (ultimate statement).

Some jñāna are bādhitajñāna;

i.e., The jñāna, which gets sublated, replaced, or negated by other jñāna like 'sunrise and sunset.' We all know that the sun never rises or sets, but we are used to believing otherwise from childhood onwards. But this jñāna gets replaced once we come to know that the sun never rises or sets. In vyavahāra, we still use the former jñāna, but we never get deluded by it anymore. Likewise, if we know each and everything's nature, we give it its proper place in vyavahāra. And then we never get carried away by its impermanent nature. However, we use it according to the vyavahāra (which takes place in our day-to-day life), and hence we are free from its bondage.

nāsha of Vritti:

After hearing Satsang, we forget it because the nature of the vritti is to undergo modifications continuously. It gets destroyed (nāsham) and thus cannot stay as the same vritti because its nature is utpatti (creation) and nāsha (destruction). So when you are not listening to a Satsang or when you are involved in other activities, other vrittis replace the Satsang vritti and you begin to think accordingly.

Manana - reflecting

"One should see hardships in life as stepping stones to success. Self-confidence will help one to break free from the impurities and bondage of the mind and allow one to soar to the heights of spirituality." -Amma

To get rid of the doubts regarding one's true nature, one needs to keep reflecting on Guru's words and Shastra's words. We got to know ourselves as 'sat' when we listened to upadēśam - so jñāna utpatti happened already. However, we are not able to sustain the conviction arising from that jñāna. This is because the impression of concepts arising from the words heard during Satsang (shravaṇa) is weak compared to body-mind samskāra (our impressions regarding ourselves and the world). The latter overpowers sharvaṇa samsakāra leading to doubts in words heard during Satsanga. The only way out is to intensify the Satsang samskāra. When Satsang samskāra becomes strong, then it will overpower other samskāras –This is mananaphalam, through repeated shravaṇam.

This overpowering happens because antahkaraṇam has three dośas (impurities)

Maladośa is gross impurities as punya, pāpa. This goes away by doing Karma yoga, which in turn leads to chittashudhi.

Vikṣepadośa is the distraction of the mind. This goes away by upāsana –dhyāna, archana, japa, etc., which leads to citta ekagrata.

Avaraṇadośa is a veil of ignorance covering Atma, so we say, 'I do not know Brahman' (Atma). If Brahman is there, I should be able to see it. Since it is not seen, Brahman is not there at all. Such a doubt gets cleared by knowledge about our real 'sat' nature—as 'I am sat.'

Nididhyāsana

"Keep a close watch on the mind! It is a clever liar that stops you from being aware of your true nature, the Self." -Amma

Repeated hearing and clearing doubts to get conviction about one's true nature with the help of Śruti and Guru, by getting rid of vipareeta bhavana, i.e., all thoughts that make one think 'I am body...'.

Difference between shravaṅajñāna and other types of knowledge happening day to day in our activities;

Let us first look at some other types of knowledge to understand the difference between these and shravanajñāna

Pratyaksha jñāna: The knowledge that happens due to our senses is called pratyaksha jñāna; Knowledge of a 'thing' happens when our senses come in contact with objects, e.g., when eyes come in contact with a pot in front, we will have pot knowledge. Likewise, when all other indriyas come in contact with respective things, we will have the jñāna accordingly. However, atmajñāna cannot be revealed because of indriyas, because indriyas themselves get revealed by Atma.

Anubhava jñāna (Experiential knowledge) - Whatever experiential knowledge we acquired by anubhava of seeing a pot, a table, etc., can be forgotten or remembered. But atmajñāna is not something we acquire through some vishaya (objective) anubhava and, at the same time, not subject to forgetfulness or remembrance. It is always nithya siddha vasthu.

Paroksha-jñāna (Indirect knowledge): For example, we hear about the Himalayas. Based on the information we hear, we will have some knowledge about the Himalayas. Still, it is only indirect knowledge since we have never actually been there. However, Atma jñāna is not a kind of knowledge that you can get by collecting or acquiring information about Atma, like in the case of paroksha-jñāna.

Aparoksha-jñāna (Direct knowledge): For example, after hearing about the Himalayas, if one wishes to go to the Himalayas, then he has to travel a certain distance to reach the Himalayas. Once he reaches the Himalayas, he will have direct knowledge of the Himalayas. But since Atma is not divided by time and space, one does need to travel in space or time to achieve atmajñāna because it is one's nature.

sākshibhasyam: Sakshi, the witness self, means 'that' which is illumining the antahkaraṅa and is also the substratum for antahkaraṅa, e.g., a canvas illumines the images that appear on it and is also the substratum of all those images. Sometimes in our antahkaraṅa (predominantly mind), we will experience happiness, misery, anger, jealousy, etc.... Here we don't need indriyas or other types of pramāṅas like pratyaksha pramanam (due to senses), shabda pramaṅa (due to sound in the form of words), anumāna pramāṅa (due to inference), or other types of pramaṅams to say that we are experiencing sukha or dukha. This is because antahkaraṅa appears in ćaitanyam (Consciousness). Antahkaraṅa is born from sattva guna of pancha mahabhutas and hence has this special quality of reflection. So ćaitanya gets reflected in antahkaraṅa. Now antahkaraṅa also appears as if it is chinmāyam (conscious). Because of this reflective power, all the experiences (including thoughts) seem to be illuminated by antahkaraṅa, just like the mirror reflecting the sunlight illuminates a dark room. Antahkaraṅa continuously undergoes modifications, but we get to know all the thoughts that pass through antahkaraṅa immediately because these modifications are illuminated by the Sakshi ćaitanya (Witness self). Therefore all objective appearances include illusionary things like mirages, snake in a rope and rope. Then subjective states of the mind like happiness, misery etc. and ignorance are revealed by sākshibhāsyam. Atmajñāna is not illuminated by any other jñāna, just like Sun does not need candlelight to be illuminated.

Phalavyāpti (Resulting knowledge): All cognition(vrittis) arises from antahkarańa and hence is also permeated with ćaitanya. This phenomenon is called vritti abhāsa ćaitanyam. When the vritti goes out through the eyes, it uncovers the object in front of us, and at that time, we come to know the 'this-ness' of the object. For example, when the abhāsa ćaitanya in the vritti illumines the object in front of us, then we say 'this is a pot, table' etc....Such knowledge is called phalavyāpti. The same thing happens in the case of other indriya vishaya jñāna. In both cases, jñāna is kāraka, i.e., resulting from vrittis.

Shravana jñāna and its phala

"Within you, immense knowledge is waiting for your permission to unfold." -Amma

When we are doing shravańa(listening to scriptures or Guru's words) like 'tat tawamasi,' 'Atmaswarūpam thou art,' 'premaswarūpam thou art,' – the vritti arising out of shravana goes and destroys the ignorance 'I am not sat' or 'I am not Atmaswarūpam' or ' I am not premaswarūpam.' In that process, this vritti also gets destroyed. Then the 'sat' 'Atmaswarūpam' shines by itself, as by nature it is self-effulgent. Thus it does not require the help from abhāsa ćaitanya to shine, just as the sun does not require any help from a candle to shine or sun rays are not needed to illuminate the sun itself. This is vrittivyāpti, not phalavyāpti. Hence jñāna is jnāpakam, i.e., knowledge is pointing to what our real nature is. It is not kārakam (resulting knowledge).

When heard with the help of Guru, this Atmajñāna will bear the phala, i.e., you will know yourself as Atmaswarūpam, Premaswarūpam. In Gita, Krishna says unreal nature is 'Agamāpayinah (have a beginning and an end), anityāh (transient).' So, 'forebear pair of opposites like 'happiness and misery,' 'heat and cold,' 'victory and defeat," gain and loss,' 'comfort and hardship,' etc.

'All that is born will die. As the body came, so too, it will go. But the Atma was never born. Therefore, it is everlasting - eternal.'

'That which is 'sat' 'never ceases,' that which is 'asat' 'can never be' (as permanent, real). So knowing these two natures 'as such,' the wise ones are free.'

Conclusion

"We should live every moment with awareness." -Amma

Amma's every word, movement, gesture flows from that brahmanishtha standpoint only. So we have to come to that state by realizing our true nature by cherishing Amma's presence through her darshan, by her smiles, by her service, by her Love and Compassion and by her Atmanishtha upadēśa.

ॐ

Appendix

The Great Awakening-letter to satsang group on New Year 2022

"The Divine is present in everyone, in all beings, in everything. Like space it is everywhere, all pervading, all powerful, all knowing." -Amma

Om Namah Shivaya.

May the Divine bestow all of you with good health, wealth, contentment, peace, and prosperity.

Best wishes for the new year. Remembering the ancient lineage of Rishis, I pray to the Guru parampara that the Lord, Guru grant to you all prosperity, health, and mental peace in the New Year.

As we all know, it has been two years since the COVID pandemic, and the impact on our lives and the economic impact on the world has been tremendous. My deep condolences to those who died due to this COVID and other ailments. Everyone is distressed by having to stay indoors during all this time. There are difficult life situations and mental disturbances, which seem significant. Whenever there is a crisis like this or any other challenging situation in life, we are swayed by our emotions and the whims and fancies of our minds.

We are entangled in the snares of saṃsāra.

"Don't try to become what you are not; You are already what you are." So let the wisdom of Atma, the Self become your priority and be peacefully content appreciating this Truth.

This wisdom says one is not body, mind, and thoughts, as they are known, and that which knows is the pure awareness of Self. Thus being the very consciousness, one cannot become any other thing. Instead, shine all the objective appearances as they are. Atma, the Self, is all the reality which one is.

If this is the Truth, then how does one become an aspirant for this Truth, and how does one realize this Truth?

In this world, one is trying to become complete, starting with naming the baby, the idea of perfection starts. Parents try to give a perfect environment for studying to get a good job and have a family. Therefore with the idea of fullness in life, one begins the journey to achieve that. Therefore everyone is behind something in the world in order to fill the gap of incompleteness. Also one wants to be satisfied mentally to remain peaceful. Thus intellectually, emotionally one tries to achieve this with a good diet, exercise, yoga, etc. In this way, others seeking mental and physical happiness, they start exploring by going to places, meeting people, and developing relationships. All want a healthy way of life to satisfy the desire to become content.

Eventually few come or turn inwards; this is spirituality. To become fully content, they come to this path learning there is no completeness, peace in outside things even though they achieved them in different proportions. Thus, the inward journey begins. The birth of an aspirant for realizing this Truth starts. Then follows an enquiry on how to arrive at this Truth.

Slowly learns about the masters who have achieved this feat. They Read their books and become inspired. Then one wants to meet those wise men. Thus one comes to master and pursues a life of peace and happiness. The aspirants then do selfless service and concentrate their mind on Self.

Thus to gain more understanding in this path, one hears Upanishad words such as 'Tat twam asi' (Thou are that) and comes to the Self, which is the nature of everything.

The 'Tat' means the reality, Brahman. 'Thou' means the one who is hearing or reading these words. 'Asi' means the hearer of this Truth is Brahman himself, not any more individual with name-body-mind-intellect complex. Brahman is absolute existence, absolute consciousness, and absolute bliss. 'Thou' the Atma is Brahman himself. But various doubts arise regarding Brahman as Self after we hear this scripture and Guru telling the Truth.

'I am body,' I am mind.' How can I be Brahman (The Self)? (Known as Viparyayam in vedanta)

I have my own thoughts, sensations, perceptions, and feelings and feel elated or depressed continuously without rest. If so, how can I be "That" ?

Is Atma one or many? If it is "one" how is it I see many people with many things around?

I am so miserable sometimes. I don't know that 'I am Atma' as said in the scriptures. This knowledge seems contrary. (Known as Ignorance in Vedanta)

So before one realizes this Truth clearly, one starts to question the master as above. The master explains with an analogy of the screen.

The screen analogy

One aspirant asked, "How to appreciate Atma despite all the conflicts around and in my mind? How to arrive at this Truth very easily and realize Atma is me and everything?"

Answer:

How do we see the screen when all pictures appear and cease continuously?

The screen is no more in our sight. Only pictures with all the scenery, people, and their emotions are seen to be continuously following one another. All these appearances take over and overpower us with excitement. Thus we build relationships with each appearing character and fight with our emotions in the mind which are nothing but appearances.

Now for us the foreground is a continuously changing pictures only, and the screen is not even considered. Here the most important observation we have to note is, how can we miss screens altogether which is the most obvious fact. That's the power of māya, the illusion. That which is the most obvious thing is missed, and that which appears and ceases is given full priority. This confusion is also called Superimposition (Adhyāsa).

How does the screen remain a mystery? And we don't try to look and understand all the while when pictures appear and cease. Do we have to search for the screen in each appearance and try to appreciate it? Or is the screen not at all present? All confusion comes in this lack of understanding, and we fail miserably. This is a sorrowful state because we try to limit the screen to one picture or an appearance. This mistaken identity is the birth of ego or limited self. That is, we try to limit the screen to an appearance. At the same time, the screen is free of all appearances.

This type of mistaken identity leads to a search where appearances try to grab the screen! This endless search is like trying to climb on one's own shoulders, which is impossible.

If we enquire why this happens, then we will know it is because of a lack of discernment between the screen and appearances. Even though the screen is both the background and foreground, we are completely lost in the bewildering appearances! Thus, we must have the proper knowledge to overcome these confusion. With this understanding, we can discard what is not reality and come to reality. The most apparent foreground is the screen, and never ever it can cease, and the same is the background for all appearances. Though appearances on-screen seem apparent to our eyes, it is only for some time as they cease. The screen, all the while, is there in every appearance as one whole truth. Whereas appearances all the while, even though they seem 'as if' they are there independently, in fact, are not. This is because they get negated when one appearance replaces the other. Thus continuously, they change to give place for new appearances. Therefore the screen is the content and substratum for all appearances. Moreover, the screen is most direct and immediate compared to appearances which are indirect and not immediate in nature. Therefore they appear and cease all the time.

The screen is the presence, and all appearances take that light of presence to show up. In that presence, all appearances get the effulgence and seem 'as if' they are the foreground, but they are only dancing on the screen. Thus most obvious is the screen, which is not meant to be searched instead realized. Therefore, even though all appearances on the screen appear, the screen never gets distorted or distributed.

Thus the reality of the screen is ever free of all appearances. There are no real appearances on the screen to say we are missing the screen. Thus we see clearly the screen when all pictures appear and cease continuously without any more ignorance, doubts, and contrary thinking, considering them as reality. This clarity is all the Truth. With this clarity and discernment of mind the screen is seen despite all appearances. It is understood that in each and every appearance, it is screen alone; hence there was no cessation of the screen at any point in time. Whichever picture we try to touch, we are only touching the screen all the time.

In the first step, discernment brings in the understanding that the screen is the reality and pictures are unreal because they share the reality of the screen for their appearance. With this understanding, dispassion arises towards unreal appearances.

In the second step, discernment shows that pictures are not different from the screen. With this understanding, dispassion becomes more focused and appreciates the screen with less conflict.

In the third step, one realizes everything is the screen only. If anything other than the screen is seen, it is understood that it is just an appearance without reality. Now the dispassion becomes natural as there is nothing to discard as everything is the screen itself.

"Therefore, to appreciate the screen despite all things appearing and going around without our mind becoming disturbed needs discernment about the screen. This brings our attention to the screen. The screen is one, but we think the screen is many, or there is no screen due to the eclipse of appearances. We don't have any idea about the screen in childhood even though our parents tell us. Slowly when we develop discernment, we arrive at this truth. Then very easily, we understood the screen was there all the time, but our focus was on pictures. Thus the reality of all appearances is that the screen alone is realized very easily."

Similarly, How do we realize Atma the Self when body-mind-world complexes appear and cease continuously?

Atma, the Self, is not in our experience; instead, only the body-mind-world complex with all its continuously changing emotions and wonders follow one another. All appearances of the body-mind-world complex take over and overpower us with excitement. Thus we build relationships with each individual and fight with our emotions in the mind which are nothing but appearances.

Now for us, the foreground is body-mind-world complex only, and Atma, the Self, is not even considered. Here the most important observation we have to note is how can we miss Self which is the absolute Existence, Consciousness. That's the power of māya, the illusion. That which is the most apparent thing is missed, and that which appears and ceases is given full priority. This confusion is also called Superimposition (Adhyāsa).

Where is Atma the Self? It remains a mystery, and we don't try to look for it. Do we have to search for Atma the Self in each appearance and try to appreciate it? Or is Atma not at all present? This confusion arises in this lack of understanding. Thus we fail miserably. This is a sorrowful state because we try to limit the Atma to one individual body-mind complex. This mistaken identity is the birth of ego or limited self.

That is, we try to limit Atma the Self to an individual. Whereas Atma the Self is free of all body-mind-world complex appearances. These appearances challenge to show Atma the Self 'as if' it is there within limited self reach! This type of mistaken identity leads to a search where individual appearance tries to grab the Atma! This endless search is like trying to climb on one's own shoulders, which is impossible.

If we enquire why this happens, then we will know it is because of lack of discernment about Atma the Self and body-mind-world complex appearances. Even though the Atma is background as substratum and foreground as noumenon, we are completely lost in the bewildering body-mind-world complex appearances! Thus, we must have the proper knowledge and come out of this confusion. With this understanding, we can discard what is not reality and come to reality. The most apparent foreground is the Atma the Self, and never ever it can cease, and the same is the background for all appearances. Though appearances on Atma the Self seem obvious to our eyes, it is only for some time as they cease in time. The Atma is unsublated Awareness, and all the while is there in every appearance as one whole Truth. Whereas appearances all the while, even though they seem 'as if' they are thereby themselves are not. The body-mind-world complex has no independent reality of its own.

They get negated (sublated) when one appearance replaces other appearances. Thus continuously, they change to give place for new appearances. Therefore Atma the Self is the content and substratum for all appearances. Atma the Brahman is most direct and immediate compared to indirect and not immediate appearances. Consequently, they appear and cease all the time. The Atma, the Self, is the presence, and all appearances take that light of presence to show up. In that presence, all appearances get the effulgence of Self and seem 'as if' they are the foreground. Still, they are only appearances on the Atma the Self. Thus most obvious is the Atma the Self, which is not meant to be searched for instead, realized as it is. Therefore even though the body-mind-world complex appear on Atma the Self, but never Atma, the Self gets distorted or distributed.

Thus the reality of the Atma the Self is ever free of all appearances. There are no real appearances on the Atma the Self to say we are missing Self. Thus we see clearly Atma the Self when all body-mind-world complexes are appearing and cease continuously without any more ignorance, doubts, and contrary thinking, to take them as reality. Thus I am body; I am mind etc., cease. This clarity is all the Truth we have when our discernment mind shows the Atma the Self despite all appearances. Brahman alone is understood in every appearance. Hence, there is no cessation of Atma the Self at any point in time. Whatever thoughts, sensations, perceptions, and feelings that arise are nothing but Atma the Self. We are only appreciating this Truth all the time. In the light of Atma, the Self all gets revealed.

In the first step, discernment shows that Atma the Self is the reality and the body-mind-world complex is unreal. Because they share the reality of Atma, the Self for their existence, thus, dispassion arises towards the unreal body-mind-world complex of appearances.

In the second step, discernment shows that the body-mind-world complex is not different from the Atma the Self. With this understanding, dispassion becomes more focused. As a result, one appreciates Atma the Self with less conflict, which arises as thoughts, sensations, perceptions, and feelings.

In the third step, one realizes everything is Atma only. If anything other than Atma is seen, it is understood that it is just an appearance without reality. Thus when one hears about Atma, the Self is the Self of all, a firm conviction arises with the repeated reflection. This conviction brings the realization that in Self, there is no misery, latent impressions, or mind with conflicts. Now the dispassion becomes natural as there is nothing to discard as everything is Atma the Brahman itself.

"Therefore, appreciating Atma the Self in spite of thoughts, sensations, perception, and feelings without becoming disturbed needs knowledge based discernment. This brings our attention to Atma the Self. The Atma is one, but due to many-ness in appearances, we think the Atma the Self as many or there is no Atma in the first place. We don't have any idea about Atma the Self in general as we are not told about this Truth. We slowly become aspirants to know this Truth, and when we approach the master and listen to the words like 'Thou art that' 'Your Self is Awareness.' With the sword of discernment, we arrive at this Truth. Then very easily we understand that Atma the Self is there all the time as our very nature, but our focus was on the body-mind-world complex. The reality of all appearances is the Atma the Self. Thus everything is Brahman alone.

Therefore as said in the quote holds good. "Don't try to become what you are not; You are already what you are." So let the wisdom of Atma the Self become your priority and become peacefully content as you are already that.

As in the Tenth Man story, The Tenth Man was looking for the Tenth Man! Similarly, we are all knowers of Self (Tatva Jnanis) who think of ourselves as aspirants (Mumukshus) and trying to search for Self. Being Atma the Self, we are looking for it! This Satya, Atma, is my True Nature and nature of everything.

May everyone arrive at such Tattva jñāna this year is my sincere wish.

Om Namah Shivaya.

Swami Amritachitswarūpananda Puri.

Spiritual progress through Guru's words

"Living with Mother is like being in an airplane as it moves on its way to the take-off point. First the airplane moves slowly out of the airdrome towards the runway; it then moves faster and faster along the runway until it finally takes off. If one learns to live in Mother's presence with an attitude of love and self-surrender, it will certainly bring one to the take-off point. In Mother's presence you do not remain the same—you are constantly changing internally. The old patterns disappear as you move deeper and deeper into the new realms of your true existence."
-Amma

All of us have decided to walk on the spiritual path. You could say that it is due to God's grace or Guru's grace. We have come to understand that there is really no true happiness in this world. However great our achievements in this world may be, we understand that one does not find fulfillment in this world. But walking on the spiritual path does not mean coming to or living in an ashram. It is really about the spiritual enquiry within.

Our focus should really be on our true nature -'Who am I?.' One can be a young student, or a householder doing her daily job, a sanyasi in an ashram, or a person leading a retired life. The stage of life or kind of job one is engaged in, matters little. The essential thing though is to adjust our life situation such that it does not interfere with our spiritual progress.

Spirituality is not about trying to live a poor life, or doing things like eating just rice gruel, sleeping on the floor, eating sparingly or wearing a certain type or color of clothes,etc. It is not just about practicing austerities or living a simple lifestyle. In the olden days, spiritual aspirants used to go to the forest or beg for food in villages. However those practices should not be our focus in the present times.

Spiritual aspirants today are very much in touch with society whether we live in an ashram or at home. Changing one's location has not changed the link with society. There is really no need to give up our jobs or other worldly responsibilities. Where we stay, what we eat, what we wear and so on is not an obstruction to our spiritual life, as long as we focus on our real internal nature, rather than on external aspects of life.

We need to earn an income to maintain a family or to practice charity like supporting an ashram through donations. So earning income through honest, truthful means is not wrong. Eating poorly, fasting, avoiding sleep or other physical hardships is not spirituality. Neither does eating healthy food with adequate amounts of protein and so on go against spirituality.

On the spiritual path we reflect on who or what is God or reality. Before embarking on our spiritual path, we had a mental concept about what God is. Each religion has its own practices, rituals and beliefs. But the deep thinkers or spiritual philosophers such as Shankara, Plato or great Christian or Sufi saints, these great souls have found out the Truth and experienced God face-to-face. They have shared these Truths with us in the form of the Mahavākyas such as 'You are That reality' (Tat twam asi). They point out that the focus should be on our real nature. They remind us that our real nature is Sat-Chit-Ananda (Being-Awareness-Bliss), that freedom (Mukti) is our real nature.

We normally think of ourselves as individuals with a body, mind, thoughts, feelings, emotions, etc. That is how we live our day-to-day life, sometimes getting angry, sometimes being impatient, being happy, being unhappy, sometimes losing our balance but other times exhibiting good behavior. Even though sometimes we feel that we are in a win-win situation despite thinking of ourselves as individuals. During other times, we experience negative states of mind and life situations which are painful.

In order to help us avoid such ups and downs, the Guru inculcates in us qualities such love, compassion and a service (seva) mindset. Through such practices, we start to attain a certain degree of evenness, purity of mind (chitta shuddhi) and attain one pointedness of mind. Guru then points out that we need to move further from our external focus to an internal focus.

Mental purity (chitta shuddi) by itself is not enough to know the Truth. Our spiritual practices help us to know the Truth but they are not the Truth. We might spend all our time in spiritual practices like Japa, Sevas, Bhajans, Pujas, spiritual talks etc but they are not an end in themselves. Our spiritual practices must ultimately help us with the realization of our True nature. In general, external practices are like keeping a spring compressed with our fingers. Ultimately, we remove our hand when our hand begins to hurt. Similarly practices are not the end in themselves. We might feel we have a certain degree of control over our minds through such practices, but if we ease up on the practices, the mind will return to its old patterns. So, while we continue to perform our spiritual practices, we should also start focusing on understanding who we really are, our essential nature.

So these practices help us to gain clarity of the mind but we have to take the next step after achieving this one-pointedness of the mind. This next step is to inquire into the Truth and to understand what our real nature is. This is the focus of the Upanishads. Their focus is on our real nature. The real nature of the inquirer, the spiritual seeker.

We have forgotten our real nature and got drowned in the ocean of worldliness (samsāra). In the story of the tenth man, the tenth man felt sad because he believed one in the group was lost, since he only could count nine others in the group. When the tenth man is told that he himself is the tenth man, he is able to drop his sadness. Similarly the Upanishad says that we are that Brahman or the universal Self. We are That which we have been looking for all this time.

It is really having the conviction that we are really Brahman. Being always the Universal Self, we forgot our real nature and think of ourselves as individuals. The Upanishads remind us that our real nature is the Universal self. The aim of the Guru is to convey to us the truth about our real nature.

In most traditions, spiritual practices often adopt a certain attitude to assist in worship (upāsana). For example, in the Hindu tradition, a Saligram stone (smooth stone from the Gandaki river) is treated as a symbol of Vishnu and people worship it. Even though it is only a smooth stone we view it as a symbol of Vishnu and perform upāsana. Similarly, If we grew up as a Hindu, we view God as Vishnu, Shiva or Kali, Ganapathi, etc. We pray to them, converse with them and we make promises to them. All these practices help us to purify and gain clarity of mind.

Similarly, many feel that the good things in life are due to the grace of God (Ishwara) or Guru. Millions of people visit temples like Tirūpathi or Palani because they get peace and fulfillment by visiting these spiritual places. It is their faith in these spiritual places that give them peace. What is really happening is that such visits help us to still the mind and the Self is reflected in that stillness.

In our relationship with the Guru, it is similar. We adopt a certain attitude and see the Guru as the symbol of God and perform puja to the Guru. We see all the Gods embodied in the Guru. We do Guru pada seva, serve the Guru and in every way see the Guru as God. All these are helpful in creating mental purity and one-pointedness of mind. When Amma hugs us or when Amma looks at us, in that instant our mind becomes still and we feel fulfilled. We pray to God or the Guru intensely through bhavana (by strongly feeling that Guru is a symbol of God), we achieve these benefits which still our mind for a short duration. After gaining this one-pointedness of mind, we need to take the next step of finding out 'what is my real nature? Who am I?'

How should I find out my real nature? How can I gain a firm conviction about the Truth? First I have to understand that my current problems exist because of an incorrect understanding of self, and that I have a real nature beyond this individual nature. The Guru tells us that our real nature is Atman or Brahman. When the disciple asks the Guru, 'please teach me the Truth,' the Guru tells us our real nature is That pure reality and that we are never different from that Brahman at any time. The Guru here is speaking about the nature of the disciple (the one who is asking the question and listening to the Guru) which is Brahman itself.

Our Upanishads say that when the disciple asks the Guru, or similarly when Maitreyi asks her sage husband Yagnavalkya, or when Svethaketu asks his father Uddalaka, or when Nachiketa asks Yama the God of death, these great spiritual gurus are really conveying our real nature to us (the nature of the one who is asking). The Amrita Tatvam (the Truth that makes us immortal) is being explained to us by these great teachers. The Guru has great wisdom about our real nature. When we ask such mahatmas, please teach me so that I can also be in the same blissful state (anandaswarūpam) as you, they convey the Truth to us so that we may become free from our perceived bondage.

Most of us see the Guru as God and keep the Guru in great reverence. Just like we respect a PM or a President, we normally view the Guru as an individual and offer our deep respects. Just as we think of ourselves as a person, we think of the Guru as a person. The difference between the Guru and the ordinary person is that the Guru has knowledge of the Self. The true nature of both the Guru and the disciple is the same. We should see the Guru as the one who can convey the Truth about our real nature and approach such a mahatma and ask her - 'please teach me and help me gain that status that you are in so that I also can be in that state of Ananda.' Then through compassion the Guru tells the disciple how he/she can attain the same status by becoming aware of their true nature.

Let us take the example when Vivēkananada asks Sri Ramakrishna about his spiritual experience. When Vivēkananda questions Sri Ramakrishna whether his experience of the Truth is just specific to him or if it was attainable by anyone else. Sri Ramakrishna immediately answers saying that anyone can attain his state and asks vivēkananda if he wants to get that experience. So the main interest of the Guru is to convey the Truth that she has experienced to the disciple through teaching by word of mouth. So we really have to focus on the message that the guru is conveying. We have to see the Guru as the Truth she is conveying and not as an individual. We normally see the guru as an individual with a human body and mind and thus limit the guru. Here, the Guru is not a person but the Truth that she is conveying to the disciple about the real nature of the disciple. Our focus should be on the message that the Guru is conveying.

Our focus should be on Guru's words that tell us that our real nature is ever-present, ever-pure, ever-awareness and ever free (Nitya, Śuddha Buddha Mukta). Through the guru's instruction (upadēśam) we need to understand that our real nature is that unchangeable reality. Our focus has to shift from Guru's physical form to the message conveyed by the guru that we are Sat-Chit-Ananda (Being-Awareness-Bliss). That is why Sri Shankara says 'Guru naiva Shisya' - neither Guru nor Disciple. The meaning here is that we should focus on the Truth taught by the Guru and not on viewing the Guru and disciple as individuals.

We notice that Amma addresses us by first saluting us as embodiments of love (premaswarūpa), embodiments of Brahman (atma swarūpa). Amma sees us as atman and not as individuals, and uses every opportunity to remind us of our essential nature. That Atma, which is ever Pure and Free (Nitya śuddha Mukta) is you. Guru converts the Upanishad into a vocal instruction. Ultimately through God's grace (Iswara kripa, Guru kripa) we will understand that everything around us is God. So with God's grace, Guru's grace and our own Atma's grace we have to inquire into our real nature.

Doing Guru seva is important but at the same time the focus should be turned to your real nature and not be stuck in the external practices. It is not the intention of the Guru that you should hold on to her all the time or be with her all the time. The main interest of the Guru is for you to know the Truth and understand your real nature which is the nature of everything around us and the Guru as well. With this vision we understand that this spirituality is not just in the Guru but is in every one of us. This is what we need to be convinced about our real nature. When Guru speaks, she is not speaking about herself but is reminding us that our real nature is that universal Self, the Sat-Chit-Ananda.

Wisdom related Self Q & A

The whole discussion is about recognizing the Self. We are not talking about any other thing here. There is no point in talking about others or anything else because it will not help us understand our Self. Rather, it will delude more into the world of names and forms. The inquiry of who we are in the context of the Upanishads is what we are discussing here. The Upanishadic wisdom is where the lineage of teachers and Mahatmas come and reveal to us the nature of Self.

They point all the meaning of words to us directly and tell us until our doubts get resolved. Each cult, sect, religion, culture has its own gods and goddesses. All are invited to this inquiry and to arrive at the Self. All external symbols, dogmas, holy books, images of gods are the pointers for the aspirants who are here to inquire and come back to the source of oneself and everything, the Self. That source Self is vocalized as 'I' or 'I am,' and everyone chants this all the waking time till one goes to sleep.

Q - Where does this vocalized 'I' go when one is asleep? And how does it get activated in the world?

The mind, senses, intellect resolves along with 'I' in Self, the pure existence source. Then again, as one emerges to the waking state from pure existence, the effulgence awakens and throbs. Then gets vocalized as 'I.' This 'I' then identifies with thoughts, sensations, feelings, perceptions and behaves as a body-mind complex individual in the world with all empirical activities.

Q - What is the driving force for its effulgence? And why does It does so?

It is its nature to do so. As its nature, it is ever there and will be there. As we hear these words, we are there as Self-nature without any coloring of thoughts, sensations, perceptions, feelings, and body-mind-world complex. When there is no effulgence in sleep as 'I' or during its effulgence as 'I' in waking state, Self remains ever immaculate in nature.

Q - Then why am I not aware? We are aware of many different things, but we are not aware of the source.

That's correct because we believe what we are told and embrace all the conditioning since birth. Awareness believes itself to be an individual and by grasping at what is in front of it, like thoughts, etc., and knows the world of names and forms.

Q - How are we to become aware of the source?

When the source is pointed as Self by the Master, the mind alone grasps that reality. But here, the discerning mind alone understands it. That discernment is the driving force that makes one inquire about the truth of oneself and every thing. So one becomes an aspirant of truth. To become aware of Self as it is, we need to hear the wisdom which points to one's Self as oneself and Self of all.

Q - What is the Truth?

Here the Truth is one's Self. So one has to come back and continually remember their true nature, because every time one moves away from Self when one sees, hears, smells, touches, tastes. All activities bring one to a body-mind-world complex standpoint. This makes it complicated in understanding the nature of truth along with mundane activities.

Q - When we see the common people, we will wonder how many want to know the truth?

Very few, we can say. Here, whoever reads these words becomes the aspirant of truth, the Self. Therefore our work is to come back to the source, the Self. It is not hidden inside each one. Rather, in Self, all appears, including us.

Q - Ok, what is morality's role in spirituality?

Prior to realizing the Truth, a seeker needs to relate to the body-mind complex and the world around in a manner that does not disturb oneself or society. So there are various guidelines such as the Do's and Dont's (Yama-Niyamas) and, Rituals, charity, Austerities (Yagna-Dana-Tapas). Such a moral life frees one of guilt and fear and aids the development of mental purity and focus. Such minds with fewer distractions are required to hear the wisdom. That's where moral values come in seeking the Truth, which we call a spiritual life. Ultimately righteous attitude in leading mundane day-to-day activities is helpful for one's Self-seeking path.

Q - How does one come to the final destination, and what exactly is it?

In Self realization, all words like attainment and enlightenment are not real achievements, like any other worldly attainment. It is only used figuratively. Therefore it is not a new discovery. Instead, it is the revelation of what our true nature already is. 'Who am I' is an inquiry to come to the source which is ever-present, ever-immaculate, ever-conscious, ever-free, the Satchitananda. All misconceptions which make us believe ourselves to be limited individual-self cease with this understanding. All our notions regarding who we are get sublated or negated. The ignorance regarding oneself as a bundle of thoughts, sensations, perceptions, feelings, along with the body-mind-world complex, is replaced by the knowledge of Self, which is infinite, eternal nature. Self-knowledge comes from the teaching through the lineage of teachers, where hearing one realizes the Self, which is Self of all as one Truth, this is wisdom.

Q - How does becoming aware of one's Self-nature change our lives? Why is it worth knowing one's Self-nature?

By taking ourselves to be the body-mind complex, we experience suffering because the body, mind and the world do not behave as we expect, and are often contrary to our likes and dislikes. When our self reference - that is, what one points to when they say "I" changes, their relationship to the body-mind and world completely transforms, and that's why knowing Self-nature is worth it and changes daily life. This is why it is freedom.

Swami Amritachitswarūpananda Puri

Glossary

A

Abhāsa – fallacious appearance.

Abhāsa vāda – A causation theory in non-dualistic Vedanta, which maintains that the jiva or the individual soul is an illusory appearance of the Absolute, and has no real independent status

ācharya – a spiritual guide or teacher.

adhiśthana – substratum; that upon which something rests.

advaita – not (a) two (dvaita); non-dual philosophy.

aham – I; the ego

ahankāra – egoism; the concept of Individuality

ajñāna – (spiritual) ignorance.

akṣara – imperishable; unchangeable.

anādi – without any beginning

ānanda – "true" happiness; usually called "bliss" and is an aspect of our true nature

anirvachanīya – indescribable. Used to describe the nature of māya.

anitya – transient

aparoksha – immediate or direct (relating to gaining of knowledge, i.e. does not require application of reason).

asat – non-existent; unreal

ātma – the Self; the individual Self

āvaraṅa – the veiling power of māya. See māya, Vikṣepa.

avasthā – state; usually is used in the context of one of the three states of waking, dream or sleep

avidyā – ignorance i.e. that which prevents us from realizing the Self. See also māya.

avyakta – unmanifest

B

bādha – sublation. The adjective is bādhita, meaning negated, contradictory or false.

bhakti – devotion
bhāvana – contemplation.
bheda – separation; distinction; difference;
bhrama – confusion
bodha – knowing, understanding, awareness
Brahman – the universal Self, Absolute
buddhi – intellect

C

chaitanya – consciousness, awareness.
chidābhāsa – false appearance or reflection (Abhāsa) of Awareness (chit) - i.e. the ego.
chit – Awareness; consciousness. Also see satchidananda.
chitta – the aspect of the mind responsible for memory.

D

dama – restraint over the senses; one of the six qualities that form part of Shankara's chatushtaya sampatti.
darshana – audience or meeting (with a guru); viewpoint;
deha – body
dharma – Appropriate conduct, performed with the right attitude at the appropriate time. One of the four puruShArtha-s or aims of life, according to Sanatana Dharma.
dhyāna – meditation
duhkha – pain, sorrow, trouble.

G

guńa – According to classical sāmkhya philosophy, creation is made up of three "qualities," sattva, rajas and tamas. Everything - matter, thoughts, feelings - is 'made up of' these three in varying degrees and the relative proportions determine the nature of the thing in question.
guru – One's spiritual teacher

I

Isvara – God; creator of the material universe through the power of māya.

J

jagat – the world

jāgrat – the waking state of consciousness.

japa – the repetition of a mantra;

jijñāsā – the desire to know (oneself). One who desires to know oneself; a seeker is called a jijñāsu.

jīva – the identification of the Self with a body and mind;

jīvanmukti – liberation while still living in the body

jñāna – knowledge; wisdom

Jñāni – literally, one who is endowed with knowledge; a sage; often used to refer to one who has realized the Self.

K

kalpita – fabricated, artificial; invented; supposed.

karma – literally "action" but generally used to refer to the "law" whereby actions carried out now will have their lawful effects in the future

M

mahavākya – maha means "great"; vākya means "statement." These are the pointers to the non-dual Self used in Vedanta.

manana – Reflection on what has been heard (shravana) from the guru. See also shravana, nididhyāsana.

manas – the aspect of mind acting as intermediary between the senses and the intellect (buddhi)

mantra – a syllable or a group of syllables with spiritual significance

māya – Illusion; it is the principle that brings about the illusory manifestation of the universe; it is beginningless; it is indescribable (anirvachanīya); it veils (āvarana) and projects (Vikṣepa). See also āvarana and Vikṣepa.

mithyā – Unreal; illusory;

moha – delusion; infatuation

mokṣa – liberation, enlightenment, Self-realization

mumukṣu – a spiritual aspirant with a burning desire for liberation

mumukṣutva – A strong desire to achieve enlightenment, to the exclusion of all other desires.

N

nāma-rūpa – name and form.

nāstika – atheist, unbeliever; usually refers to one who does not recognize the authority of the Vedas.

nididhyāsana – meditating on what has been heard at the time of teaching until there is total conviction. The third stage of the classical spiritual path. See also shravana and manana.

nidra – sleep.

nirodha – restraint.

nirvikalpa – without doubt

nisheda – negation, denial.

nishtha – firmness, steadiness.

nitya – eternal.

nivritti – giving up, abstaining, renouncing of desires that are contrary to the path to enlightenment.

P

paramārtha (noun); paramārthika (adj.) – the highest Truth or reality; the Absolute

paramātman – The supreme Self, Brahman, the Absolute

paramparā – tradition, lineage

prajñā – wisdom, intelligence, gnosis.

prakriti – nature, primodial nature

prāna – the vital force in the body with which we identify in the "vital sheath."

prānāyama – regulation of prana using the breath

prārabdha – Karma in action; remainder; accumulated past actions

pratyagātman – the indwelling Self

prema – love, in its pure, unselfish form (as opposed to moha).

premaswarūpam - One whose essential Self-nature is love.

purusha – Individual soul, spirit

R

rāga – attachment.

rajas – the second of the three guńa. Associated with activity and passion.

rishi – A seer or Sage.

rūpa – form, outward appearance

S

sadguru – the true teacher, a Self-realized being

sādhaka – a spiritual aspirant or, one who practices sādhana, which is spiritual discipline

sādhana – the spiritual disciplines followed as part of a path toward Self-realization

Sadhana chatuśtaya - the fourfold aid to the practice of Vedanta, these four comprise the proximate aid to Self-realization.

samādhana – contemplation, profound meditation; more usually translated as concentration; one of the "six qualities" that form part of Shankara's chatuśtaya sampatti.

samādhi – the state of total absorption and stillness achieved during deep meditation. Several "stages" are defined - see vikalpa, savikalpa samādhi, nirvikalpa samādhi and sahaja samādhi.

samsāra – the continual cycle of death and rebirth, transmigration, to which we are supposedly subject in the phenomenal world until we become enlightened and escape.

sanātana – literally "eternal" or "permanent;" in conjunction with dharma, this refers to our essential nature.

sankalpa – wish, intention, idea or notion formed in the mind

samskāra – The latent or residual impressions. Whenever an action is performed with an outcome in mind, a samskāra is imprinted in the jiva's mind. The accumulation of samskāras or tendencies dictate our nature leading people to behave in particular ways.

Sankhya - The school of philosophy founded by the sage Kapila, which professes dualistic realism with its two eternal entities Purusha (Individual Awareness) and Prakriti (Primordial matter)

sat – Existence, reality, Being, Truth. See also ananda, chit, satchitānanda.

Sat-asat - Real-unreal, Being-non Being

satchitānanda – the most commonly used word in Vedanta to describe our true nature, It translates as Being-Awareness-Bliss

satsanga – association with the good; keeping "holy company"

sattva – Pure, Steady, goodness, illuminating. It is the highest of the gunas, one of the three qualities. See guna.

shama – literally tranquility, absence of passion but more usually translated as mental discipline or self-control; one of the shamādi Shatka sampatti or "six qualities" that form part of the Sadhana chatuśtaya.

shamādi shatka sampatti – the six qualities that form part of the sadhana chatuShTaya sampatti. These are shama, dama, uparati, titikṣa, samādhAna and shraddha.

Shankara – 8th Century Indian philosopher responsible for firmly establishing the principles of Advaita.

shāstra – Scripture, teaching, doctrine, which are the sacred books on Indian philosophy

shraddha – faith, trust or belief (in the absence of direct personal experience) - the student needs this initially in respect of what he is told by the guru or reads in the scriptures.

shravaṅa – listening to the teachings of Vedanta from a qualified teacher. See also manana, nididhyāsana.

śruti – refers to the Vedas, incorporating the Upanishads. Literally means "what is heard" by the seers, the rishis. **spandana** - modulation or subtle vibrations, for example waves on water **sushupti** – the deep-sleep state of consciousness. **svabhāva** – one's natural disposition. **svadharma** – one's own dharma. **svarūpa** – the embodiment, or one's own nature (rūpa means 'form'); e.g., premaswarūpam (embodiment of love)

T

tamas – the "lowest" of the three gunas. Associated characteristics such as inertia and laziness.

Tattva jñāna - The knowledge of the Self, Self-realization

tyāga – renunciation

tapas – austerity

titiksha – forbearance or patience; one of the "six qualities" that form part of Shankara's chatuṣtaya sampatti.

turīya – literally the "fourth" state of consciousness. It refers to the non-dual reality, the background against which the other states (waking, dream and deep sleep) arise. It is our true nature. The other three states are mithya.

U

upādhi – Limiting adjunct

upanishad – "to sit close by devotedly," the last portion of the Vedas

uparama or uparati – desisting from sensual enjoyment; one of the "six qualities" that form part of Shankara's chatuṣtaya sampatti.

upāsana – worship, homage, used to refer to practices such as chanting, Japa and meditation on a deity, etc

V

Vairāgya – detachment; dispassion; nonattachment

vāsana – latent tendencies; conditioning;
Vedānta – literally "end" or "culmination" (anta) of the Vedas focused on the topic of liberation and the nature of the Absolute
vikalpa – doubt, uncertainty or indecision.
Vikṣepa – the "projecting" power of māya.
vivēka – discrimination; the function of buddhi, having the ability to differentiate between the unreal and the real.
vyakta – manifested, apparent, visible, perceptible to the senses as opposed to avyakta - transcendental.
vyavahara (noun) vyavaharika (adj.) – the relative, practical, or phenomenal world of appearances; as opposed to pāramārthika (reality) and pratibhāsika (illusory).

Y
yoga – union; a process or a path leading to the realization of oneself as the seer, commonly used to refer to the approach propagated by Patanjali

ॐ